THE STUDY GAME

THE STUDY GAME

How to Play and Win with
"Statement-Pie"

THIRD EDITION

Laia Hanau

BARNES & NOBLE BOOKS

A DIVISION OF HARPER & ROW, PUBLISHERS

New York, Evanston, San Francisco, London

To
Richard Hanau
who pushed, shoved, prodded, and browbeat
the author
until the book was done

THE STUDY GAME: HOW TO PLAY AND WIN WITH "STATEMENT-PIE." Copyright © 1972, 1973, 1974 by Laia Hanau. All rights reserved. Printed in the United States of America. No part of this book may be used or reproduced in any manner without written permission except in the case of brief quotations embodied in critical articles and reviews. For information address Harper & Row, Publishers, Inc., 10 East 53d Street, New York, N. Y. 10022. Published simultaneously in Canada by Fitzhenry & Whiteside Limited, Toronto.

First BARNES & NOBLE BOOKS edition published 1974.

LIBRARY OF CONGRESS CATALOG CARD NUMBER: 73–19948

STANDARD BOOK NUMBER: 06–463389–6

TABLE OF CONTENTS

Hello.

   I'm the Author.

This is me, myself.

I'm the part
that's writing
the book.

and this is my

other self
that fights with
the me that's
writing the book.

We can fight
about anything,

right now we've just finished
fighting about what's supposed
to be in the book,

and this is what we've decided
should go in the STUDY PROBLEMS section:

> · how to tell if you've got one.
> · why you've got it, if you have.
> · what you can do about it, if you want to.

.. You can tell that you've got a Study Problem
if you hear yourself muttering that

THE INSTRUCTOR

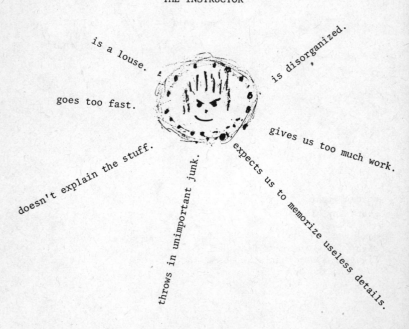

is a louse.

is disorganized.

goes too fast.

gives us too much work.

doesn't explain the stuff.

throws in unimportant junk.

expects us to memorize useless details.

You can also tell from Tests.
If you hear yourself complaining that
the Exam

. is too long
. questions are ambiguous
. has too many questions on insignificant details
. isn't fair
. doesn't let you show what you know

Or if you have a vague, miserable feeling
that there ought to be an easier way to
get through school...

.. like you're spending too much time
on school-work & still not getting
good-enough grades ??

.. like your grades are okay, but
how-cum other people get good grades
and still have time for fun & games ??

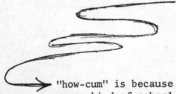

"how-cum" is because those students have worked out
some kind of school-survival study techniques...

Your first business in school is to survive, that's first.

And the business of these Statement-Pie Study Techniques
is to show you how to do it.

Now, there are two basic types of study problems. And it would probably be useful for you to know which type you've got.

After you know what you've got, and why you've got it, then learn these study techniques to cure it.

> There is absolutely no point in wasting time trying to get yourself "motivated" to study, if you don't know how to go about studying after you're motivated.

>> .. Love, affection, sympathy, guidance and motivation are no substitutes for the tools of learning.

>>> .. and neither is weeping, wailing, crying and moaning.

The two basic types of study problems are →

> The Sunburn
> &
> The Chicken-pox

The Sunburn is the all-over type.

> .. This is where school-work is a general muddle and mess, and a lot of work, and aggravation, and a nuisance or an irritation.

The Chicken-pox is the spotty one.

> .. This is where you can do one kind of school-stuff, but not another...

>> . like you can do English, but not Chemistry

>>> . or some Instructor bugs you, and you can't learn anything in his classes.

>> . or some kinds of things throw you

>>> - like in lectures ⟿

you might have trouble taking notes
and making sense out of them three
weeks later

- or in textbooks

it takes forever to read a
chapter and figure out what
it means, and what's important
in what it means ??

- or in writing things

you don't know how to fit together
all the ideas & things you thought about??

The reason   for either type

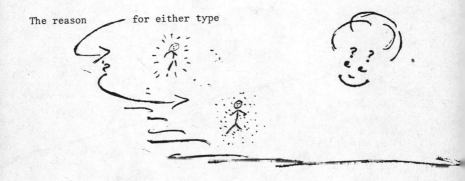

is that you really don't know

- how to do a sort-out of what's important
and what isn't, in your school stuff,
- and how to organize it,
- and, probably, how to memorize it.

You probably read your books and notes,
and discuss the stuff with friends, then
read some more...and stare out windows,
and hope that somehow everything will put
itself together in your head

which leaves the whole business of

sorting-out, organizing and memorizing
up to your Unconscious mind.

. Unconscious minds have systems for
  learning things and studying,

. but they are not very dependable
  systems. Sometimes they'll work
  and sometimes they won't.

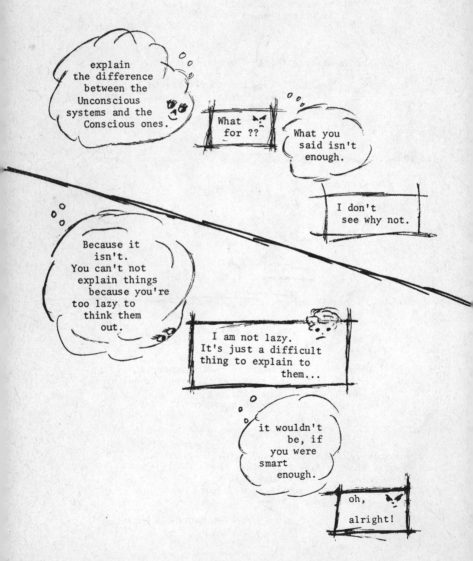

A person who has an Unconscious system for studying something,

.. he kind of reads stuff and mushes
   around, groping along and
   picking up pieces here & there,
   not knowing how to put them
   together, or if the pieces are important or not,

and sort of
   praying that somehow the whole thing
   will put itself together in his head
   by exam time.

. He gets a flickering feeling now & then
   that something inside himself is what
   puts everything together,

but he doesn't know where
the something is,
or how to make it work.

Some students like this take
up Prayer or Meditation or
grass, but they don't help...
While you are in praying or
meditating or grassing, inside

you it feels like you
Understand Everything.
But, get to the exam &
what shows up is that
the feeling was wrong.

A person who has a Conscious system for studying something,

.. knows what to do
   and when to do what
   with the different kinds of stuff
   that are in his books & classes.

And he puts it all together himself,
as he goes along in the course.

Some students like this
also take up Prayer or
Meditation or grass,
but not to help in STUDYING!

How dumb can you get??
God, your Innards & Drugs
are things for your
life-style

not for your SCHOOL-WORK!

I will give you some pictures of Unconscious study systems:

There is one that comes from never really knowing where you are in a course or when you are through studying something. It is

the

"Oh, for gawd's sakes, what's it all about anyway" system.

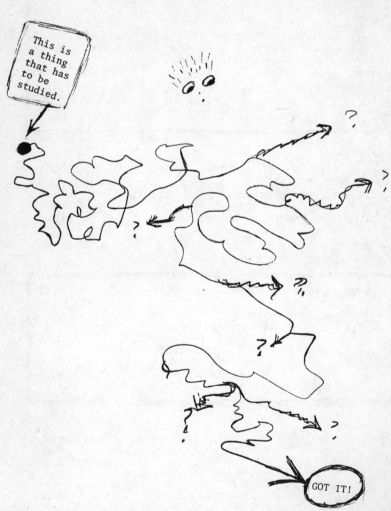

There is another one which comes from going over & over notes, underlining lines & lines in textbooks, and reading & re-reading the underlines; plus also talking & talking bits & pieces over & over with friends.

This is the

"Drowning in a Whirlpool Study System"

There is another study system...

In this one, the student feeds in material for his Unconscious mind to work with. He checks and re-checks and re-checks each piece as he goes along.

He thinks that if he understands EVERY PIECE, something inside will take over and he will understand the Whole Thing at exam time. Very time consuming. Very. And it doesn't give you the Big Picture the teachers keep asking for.

In this one, you read a paragraph
then you re-phrase the paragraph
then you re-read the paragraph
to see if you re-phrased the paragraph correctly
then you make up some questions on the paragraph
then you see if you can answer the
questions you made up on the paragraph

then I go nuts.

Because I can't stand repetition.

Paragraphs, or sections, or chapters..
I can't stand going over the same thing
five hundred thousand times!

This is the system where the mind keeps
all the clearly understood material in
separate boxes:

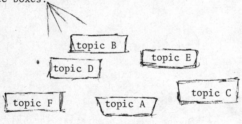

This is the

" Boxed-in Repetition System "

It can send a student into
a screeching frustration at
Exam-time.

He's translated everything into
his own words & meanings, and
he really does understand every topic,

but his Unconscious system did not
get around to ORGANIZING THE TOPICS.
Fitting them together to get the
Big Picture that the exam asked for.

His friends came to him before the exam,
and he was able to answer their questions,
and help them clear up the fuzz-areas in
their topics.

Then they all took the exam
together, and got their papers
back,

and the student let out
the Wail-of-the-Miserable-Ones

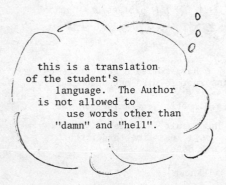

"HOW COME the damn hell he got an A
and I the damn hell get a C-plus,
when dammit I the hell TAUGHT him
the whole hell damn thing??!!*%#?!??

this is a translation
of the student's
language. The Author
is not allowed to
use words other than
"damn" and "hell".

"how come..." is because

the student did not realize that,
at every level of paragraphs, topics,

and whole courses

you have to be able to

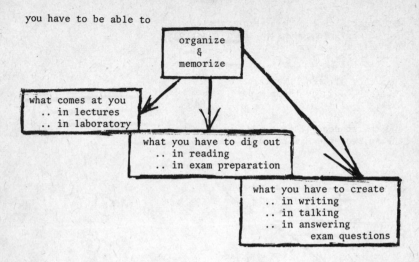

This is what School-work is.
These are the School-Think jobs you must deal with,

and Unconscious study systems often splither
into mush-puddles as you proceed through
the school system

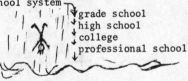

grade school
high school
college
professional school

because

. the amount of stuff you have to learn gets greater
. the repetition the Instructors dish out becomes less
  and
. the grading gets more competitive & harder on you.

The result is there's
less & less time to get the
work done...

...which lands you in the well-known
exam-time squeeze

about two days before the exam,
your Unconscious finally slops
up the brilliant plan of how
you should have studied the
course all along.

a little late.??

I am not downing anyone's Unconscious.
They are necessary and important, &
good and helpful.

But they are also lazy & undependable,
and a lot of them are sluggish.

What you need, to work easy
and survive in school

is a nice set of Conscious Study Techniques

that can show you
how to School-Think.

It is a great and sad cry of many students that
their Instructors

only want them to regurgitate facts
and don't allow them to THINK.

It is a great and sad cry of the Instructors that most
of their students

only want to regurgitate facts
and don't know how to THINK.

The Instructor is right

but the Student is not at fault.

All his life his teachers say, " THINK ! "

and never tell him how to do it.

These Study Techniques tell you.

You have to separate School-Thinking and Life-Thinking.
They are not the same thing.

You can have very useful Life-Thinking techniques
and very rotten, time-consuming School-Thinking techniques.

Thinking in school-work is
not a mystery, and it's not
a magic.

It is just a thing to learn,
like swimming, or playing
the notes on a piano.

And what teachers or Instructors call "thinking" is just a
series of mind-movements they want you to do,

for which they have many large size words
such as:
- obtaining a comprehensive overview
- learning to coordinate concepts
- conceptualization (whatever that is)
- understanding Relationships

don't let their language scare you.

School-Thinking is only a process you go through

where you fit all the facts and tidbits
they give you,

into nice, large, neat packages

and then figure out labels for
the packages.

this is
called
"studying"

and it is useful to

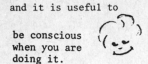

be conscious
when you are
doing it.

Statement-Pie is not only a
        Conscious system...

...it's also a Self-Checking system
        for learning things.

Any system is probably better than nothing,
but if you don't have CONSCIOUS study techniques,

Naturally, we can't get ALL the tricks of studying into
one book,

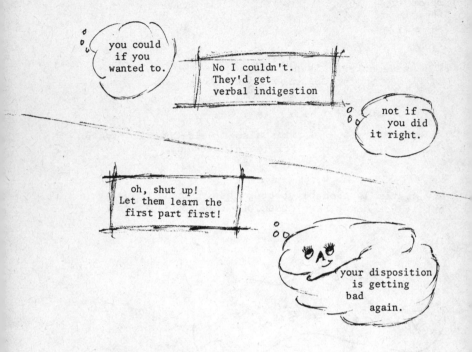

This book will cover
note-taking and organization
for textbooks and lectures.

It will put into words
what the good or brilliant student
does in his head and with his notes
when he is "studying".

Actually, there is nothing really
special about the mind of a
good student,

it just happens that a lot of
the students who get good grades

just happened to latch onto some
of the techniques for learning,
somewhere along the school line.

To learn these techniques
you can read this book.

>   Read it all the way through first,
>   if you want to.

But then you have to come back
and read each section carefully,

and practice one section
at a time.

EVERYBODY HAS TO PRACTICE.

ONE HOUR a day,
use the techniques on your school work
of that day. Use your class notes,
or textbooks or lecture notes...or all
of them.

This way you learn
the techniques AND your course
material at the same time.

smart.

very.

Begin wherever you are in your courses.
Work only on new and current material.

>   Practice only on material that
>   you are going to need for your next exam.

>   >   Find the easy pieces, and do those first,
>   >   and don't hassle the hard parts.

In a few weeks, there won't
be any more hard parts...it
just works out that way.

If you are a genius,
practice anyway. It
will help you fulfill
your genius-potential.

If you are not a genius,
as you practice...you may get
Charley-horses of the brain.

This may make you feel that
learning how to School-Think
is hard work.

It is not hard. But the mind is
only a muscle and if you have not
been exercising it
in School-Thinking (which you
probably have not been),

then you have to allow time for
some strength and power
to develop in it.

Until then,

Cut your practice period to one-half hour,
and apply the Techniques to your course work
TWICE a day.

The Charley-horses will gradually
go away.

I used
to have
Charley-horses..

After a while,

     . like your fingers automatically play the
       notes of a song you've learned,

     . like your body begins moving in the pool
       without you having to mumble,

            "..left arm forward, head to
             side, breathe, kick..
             right arm forward, head
             into water, don't breathe,
             kick.."

you've begun to School-Think.

     You've started to work easy with
     the logic and laughter of the mind

     and with the logical, laughable
     structure of knowledge.

*It's only a game -
No matter what your
teachers tell you -
School-thinking is only a game.*

THIS IS THE

NOTE-TAKING SECTION

NOTE-TAKING

The thing is

    some people know the tricks of taking notes

    but some people don't.

The result is

    some people have it easy in school

    and some people have it rough.

...which is unfair, unethical, illegal, and outrageous

and, therefore, we begin with

what every
note-taker
ought to know.

To take notes you have to know this:

EVERYTHING

written
or
spoken

IS MADE UP OF ONLY TWO ELEMENTS.

When anyone writes or
speaks he has to use
one or the other or
both. Mostly both.

I call these elements

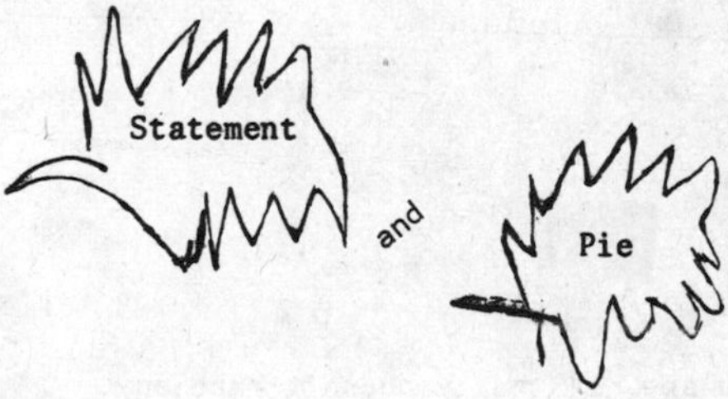

Statement

and

Pie

and the letters of P
I
E  stand for the words

P ... proof
I ... information
E ... example

But, now that you know where the letters in PIE come from,

> don't waste time figuring out whether some item is a "proof", or an "information", or an "example".

> because minds are different; and some item that you (or your Instructor) decides to call PROOF, another guy will decide to call EXAMPLE.

> .. and I'm the type who would probably call it INFORMATION.
>
> So it is easier to just call any item ⟶ Pie

You see, it really doesn't make any difference what a person thinks about any item

your mind can call any item anything it wishes

example, proof, or information ...

.. are only different words for an item.

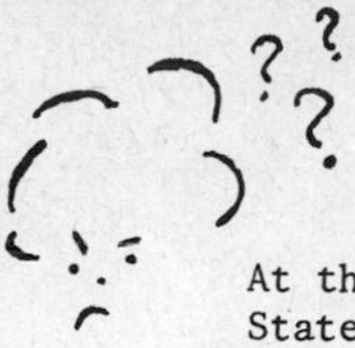

At this point you don't believe the stuff about
Statement-Pie (St-Pie)...

Anyway,
I hope you don't believe me,

since that will prove

you have a mind
not a sponge
in your head

The reason for not believing it
is that you have not been given
any proof (P)

→ that it is correct.

Nor enough information (i) about it for you to
decide whether it is true or not . . .

. . . nor enough examples (e) for you
to decide anything about anything.

So you don't accept my Statement:

"Everything, written or spoken, can be
broken into two elements: Statement & Pie"

because
you have
not been
given any
Pie for

it

which, of course, just
proves how IMPORTANT
the Pie is.

Well, it is extremely important.

Pie is the stuff that

makes someone believe what you said.

It makes your reader or listener believe your Statement.

We are not discussing
whether your Statement
is true or not. Let us
deal with first things first.

For instance: (which means the same thing as "for example")

You say to your parents: "All the kids are robbing banks this weekend."

- that is your   STATEMENT

To get your parents to believe it -- so that you can go bank robbing, too -- you name Johnny, Joe, Josephine, Bonny and Clyde who are going bank robbing.

So

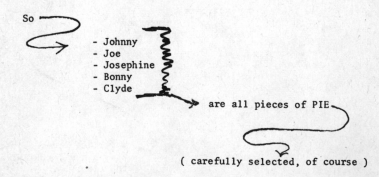

- Johnny
- Joe
- Josephine
- Bonny
- Clyde

are all pieces of PIE

(carefully selected, of course)

Another example:

You say to your parents, "But Mom-Dad, you just don't dig that all the morals in the country are changing..."

- that is your STATEMENT

Then

To get them to believe it so you can go on the weekend, too, you use

- Helen
- Hortense
- show them articles
          newspapers
          magazines
          SOME programs on TV
          SOME XX-movies

...all of which are pieces of PIE you have most carefully selected.

you note that you did not show them any items that indicated potential trouble from such weekends...??

You use Pie this way; so do your friends, and your parents...

          ...and your instructors
          and your text books

because

it works for you.

The purpose and the effect of using PIE is ⟩

to guide, direct, or control
the mind of the reader or
the listener.

This is my STATEMENT

.. now let's see if I can
get you to believe it.

... I'll use a guy named "Oscar" as my Pie

First I'll make a Statement about Oscar:

> Oscar is a very good son.

If you look into your mind,
you will see that everything
is pretty clear except that...
your mind is wavering over the
meaning of "good"

Oscar is a very good son.

Now I give you a piece of Pie for

this Statement about Oscar:

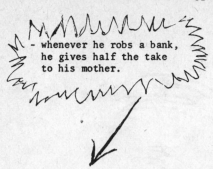

- whenever he robs a bank,
  he gives half the take
  to his mother.

Pie. And the mind snaps into focus on a particular
meaning of the word "good"

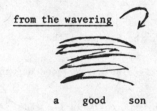

<u>from the wavering</u>

a   good   son

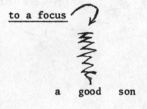

<u>to a focus</u>

a   good   son

Now, still talking about the same
guy, I make another Statement:

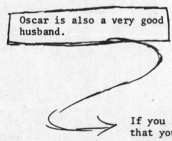

Oscar is also a very good
husband.

If you look into your mind, you'll see
that your mind is again wavering in
an arc over the word " good"

But   not   in as wide an arc this time:

first wavering

present wavering

Now I give PIE for the Statement that

Oscar is also a very good husband.

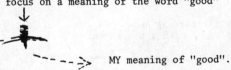

- he never strikes his wife
until he has first removed
his brass knuckles.

Pie.

And, again, what happens is...
the mind snaps into focus on a meaning of the word "good"

MY meaning of "good".

.. my meaning of "good" may seem
a peculiar meaning to you, but an idea
about Oscar...the kind of guy he is

is beginning to form in your head

because of the Pie you
have been fed about him.

Now I give you a third Statement about Oscar:

OSCAR IS A VERY GOOD FRIEND.

At this point some of you don't need any Pie about the kind
of GOOD FRIEND Oscar will be.

You wouldn't trust
him around the
corner.

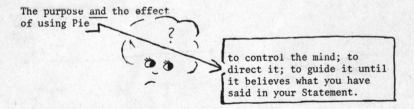

The purpose and the effect
of using Pie

to control the mind; to
direct it; to guide it until
it believes what you have
said in your Statement.

That's how it's done by advertisers, text books,
teachers, and politicians

(and you)

(and me)

Up to here I have made two Statements:

(1) Everything, written or spoken, can be broken into two elements: Statement & Pie.

(2) The purpose of Pie is to guide, direct or control the mind of the reader or listener.

At this point, you accept Statement (2)

because you were given Pie for it.

You do not, and you should not accept Statement (1)

because you have no Pie for it.

Let's have some Pie for St #1, and see what happens.

We'll use these subjects:

Math
Physics
History

Philosophy
&
Chemistry

In | Math | a STATEMENT is made:

"In order to maintain an equality, whatever you do to one side of an equation, must be done to the other side of the equation."

PIE follows

- about 10 pages of proof, explanations (information), and examples.

In [Physics] a STATEMENT is made:

"Opposite electric charges attract each other
with a force inversely proportional to the
square of the distance between them."

PIE follows

- experiments   . . | P | roof

- explanations
- applications   . . | I | nformation
- theories
- predictions

- examples   . . | E | xample

In [History] a STATEMENT is made:

"There were three causes of this war."

PIE follows

- economic causes
- geographic causes
- political causes

You begin to recognize that you can
have Pie for economic causes ???

Correct. You can,
even though economic causes
is, itself, Pie for
"There were three causes..."

Explanation coming up soon.
Patience, please.

In [Philosophy] ... which is more messy than other subjects,

We will use two philosophers:

- Philosopher A ---- Ph. A
- Philosopher B ---- Ph. B

<u>FIRST</u>

Ph. A makes a STATEMENT: "God is dead."

then he gives   PIE   to get you to believe him

216 pages of a book which gives
- proof
- arguments
- explanations
- examples

<u>THEN</u>

Ph. B. makes a STATEMENT: "Philosopher A is wrong."

<u>he</u> gives   PIE   to get you to believe him...

429 pages of a book giving <u>his</u>
- proof
- information
- examples.

<u>THEN</u>

Ph. A makes another STATEMENT:

"My learned friend, Philosopher B, is wrong."

and dishes out 1499 pages of <u>Statements & Pies</u> to get
you to believe him again.

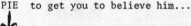

which he calls "logic"

<u>THEN</u>

you guessed it.
Ph. B gets into the act again.

This is what fills up all the shelves in the libraries.

but..I..think..we'll..
tune..out..on..them..

and switch to | Chemistry |

(St)   "Each molecule of water is composed of one atom of Oxygen and two atoms of Hydrogen."

(Pie)   6 to 16 pages of

            experiments   }   proof?
            equations

            structures
            relationships   }
            theory   information?
            reasons

Or perhaps you call one of these items "example" ?

    .your private language is your own,
    .the name-tag you give an item doesn't matter, and
    .the items are all pieces of Pie.

ANY STATEMENT

      ↪ CAN HAVE AS MANY PIECES OF PIE AS THE INSTRUCTOR OR THE BOOK HAS DECIDED TO DISH OUT.

some students don't
like this because it gives
them measles of the brain;
other students do like it
because it gives them
a smorgasbord of items
to pick from.

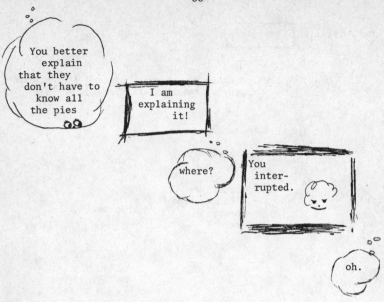

Usually, the pieces of Pie for a Statement are close by,
but sometimes they are scattered all over the place.

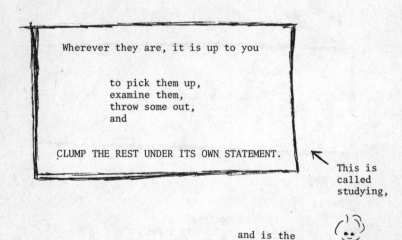

Wherever they are, it is up to you

to pick them up,
examine them,
throw some out,
and

CLUMP THE REST UNDER ITS OWN STATEMENT.

This is
called
studying,

and is the
first step
in
organizing
your material.

```
EXAMPLE
        OF STUDYING
                        where Pies
were picked up from various places
in a chapter,
                and CLUMPED.
```

ST Each molecule of water is composed of one atom of Oxygen
and two atoms of Hydrogen

CLUMP
OF
PIES
- analysis of water gives a 2 to 1 ratio
                of Hydrogen to Oxygen
- no other elements are found in water
- when Hydrogen and Oxygen gases are mixed
                in a 2 to 1 ratio, and then ignited,
                water is formed

A clump of Pies can be made up of any mixture of

proofs, examples and informations

or the clump can be
made up of ALL proofs,
or ALL examples, or
ALL informations.

                It doesn't matter.

What does matter
is that Statements
and clumps of Pie are

        put together into
        correct St-Pie Units,

                and to make these correct St-Pie Units,
                you need to understand about
                St-Pie Indents, which
                are explained next.

Rest period.

Have some milk or something.

ST-PIE INDENTS

ALWAYS indent the Pie under ITS OWN STATEMENT.

```
- Statement A
     pie
     pie        >    for Statement A
     pie

- Statement B
     pie
     pie        >    for Statement B
     pie
```

which gives you this kind
of pattern....

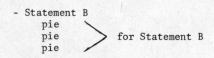

But, since you can have
Pie for Pie
        ...patience
        ...explanation coming

you can also have this kind
of pattern....

```
1 ─────────────────
  2 ───────────────
  3 ───────────────
      4 ───────────
      5 ───────────
  6 ───────────────
      7 ───────────
        8 ─────────
        9 ─────────
```

which means that:

```
2,3,6 = Pie for 1
  4,5 = Pie for 3
    7 = Pie for 6
  8,9 = Pie for 7
```

                    and since items

                        4,5 are Pie for item 3

THEN Item 3 is two things at once

> it is PIE for Statement 1
> &
> it is STATEMENT for items 4 & 5

When an item is both a Statement in the material and a Pie, it has double relationship.

ANY ITEM MAY HAVE A DOUBLE-RELATIONSHIP.

Just as you have:

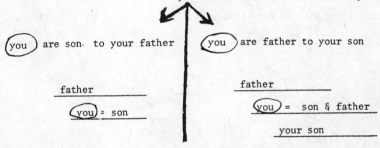

- because you are an item in the Universe,

(you) are son to your father   (you) are father to your son

father
_____

(you) = son

father
_____

(you) = son & father

your son
_____

But you are still (you) -- an item in the Universe

> your father   1
> you   2
> your son   3

item 1 = Statement for item 2

$$2 = \begin{cases} \text{PIE for item 1} \\ \quad \& \\ \text{STATEMENT for item 3} \end{cases}$$

3 = Pie for item 2

CORRECT INDENTING IS ESSENTIAL

Each piece of <u>PIE</u> must be indented under its own <u>Statement</u>

if not, you can memorize forever,
and still get low grades.

You will have memorized
Fuzz or incorrect data

which no smart student ever does.

Here's the kind of trouble you get into from incorrect St-Pieing.

The following are actual notes taken
by a college freshman during class:

"75% of the land is covered with
Sedimentary Rock. 95% of crust
is igneous."

It sounded fine to him when
he read over his notes, but
he decided to St-Pie it
anyway, just to see what
it would look like

Sedimentary Rock
- 75% of land = covered with it
- 95% of crust = igneous

Then, to indicate his versatility (i.e. show
how smart he was), he smiled and tried
out the Pie for Pie bit

Sedimetary Rock
- 75% of land = covered with it
- 95% of crust = igneous

No problems...But, it was easier to
read than the sentence -- you
could pick up the meaning quicker....
75% of the land is Sedimentary Rock.
and 95% of the.... ? ?

95% of the....

...o.k. don't panic....→ 95% of the crust of the Sedimentary
Rock is igneous?
No, it isn't...
95% of the crust of that 75% is igneous. ? ?
O.K....now, don't panic.....
..The crust of the Sedimentary Rock is igneous.
No...the crust of the LAND is igneous...

FUZZ !

@*&%#$+@*&$%#?!$!

He could see the exam question:

> WHERE IS IGNEOUS ROCK FOUND? Choose one.
>
>   (a) in sedimentary rock
>   (b) in the land
>   (c) in the crust of Sed. Rock
>   (d) in 75% of the land's crust

He could see himself seeing the exam question.

He got off his nice soft bed and went over to his desk.
He scrabbled around until he found his geology textbook. He scrabbled into the Index, hunting for crusts
and sedimentary rocks.

In his head he made unpleasant remarks about
St-Pie techniques.

He scrabbled around the pages and paragraphs,
hunting for the information that had already been
given to him in class.

        . a great and sad waste of time.

Usually speakers and books give the Statement first and Pie last, but sometimes they dish it out in opposite directions giving Pie first and Statement last, or they use the Pie-St-Pie sequence. The reasons for these last two methods is that those people like to lead up to their conclusions (which is really a Statement), or they want to give background information, or they have mixed up brains, or they were never taught to St-Pie.

.. you don't have to read that too carefully.
.. I'm going to St-Pie it for you.

```
1        Speakers
2           - Usually
3              - give ⌈St first
                      ⌊Pie last

4           - Sometimes
5              - they dish it out in opposite directions

6                 ⌈Pie first
                  ⌊St last

7              - Pie-St-Pie sequence

8           - reasons
9              - they like to lead up to conclusions
                          (conclusion = same as statement)
10             - "   want to give "background information"
11             - "   have mixed up brains
12             - "   were never taught to St-Pie
```

which gives this pattern of St-Pie indents:

- Items 2,4,5 and 8
have a double-relationship
and are both Statement & Pie

* Item 3 is NOT Pie for 1
       6 is not Pie for 4

- Item 3 is Pie for 2
       7 & 5 are Pie for 4
       6 is Pie for 5

```
1
  2
    3
4
  5
    6
7

8
  9
  10
  11
  12
```

. . . Absorption time

      which means to go do something else.

. . . Sometimes it jubbles the mind

      when school-things are simple.

rest period

..   THE   SENTENCE   CHECK-OUT   ..

a system

.. that tells if your notes are right or wrong ..

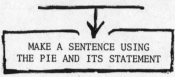

MAKE A SENTENCE USING
THE PIE AND ITS STATEMENT

If your St-Pie indents are correct, it is <u>easy</u> to make a decent sentence.

If your St-Pie indents are NOT correct, it will be a great hassle trying to put together a sentence that makes sense

and

the incorrect St-Pie will later cause you a mess of trouble due to the Eye-Mind conflict, which

you can read about now or later, on page 55

DIRECTIONS

point → to a Statement and its piece of Pie

. if there is more than one piece of Pie for a St, follow this procedure with <u>each</u> piece of Pie and the St.

. do each piece of Pie & St <u>separately</u>.

say → "This piece of Pie and its Statement is saying that ...."

fill in → the dot, dot, dots with the words that are written in your notes.

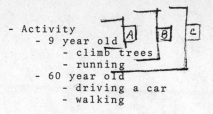

```
                   - Activity
                      - 9 year old    A    B    C
                         - climb trees
                         - running
                      - 60 year old
                         - driving a car
                         - walking
```

"This piece of Pie & its Statement is saying that
a 9-year-old has activities."   (Pie → St)   A

"This piece of Pie & its Statement is saying that
the activity of a 9-year-old is climbing trees."   B
                                  (St → Pie)

TWO THINGS TO REMEMBER FOR THE SENTENCE CHECK-OUT

---

(1)   You can read any way..... Pie → St   Pie → Pie → St
                                 St → Pie   Pie → St → Pie

it doesn't matter which way you make the sentence

"This piece of Pie and its St is saying that
running is a 9-year-old's activity." (Pie → St)   C

(2)   You can string all the St & Pies together
       into ONE sentence with 'which'es and 'that'ses

              OR you can make the St & Pies into
           SEVERAL sentences

"This piece of Pie and its St is saying that
a 60-year-old has activities, one of which
is driving a car."   (Pie → St → Pie)   ← one sentence

                        or

"This piece of Pie and its St is saying that
a 60-year-old can drive a car. Driving a
car is one of his activities."   (St → Pie → St)   ← two or more sentences

Before

St-Pie notes
BEFORE
the Sentence Check-Out

Liver functions

- important storage depot
- filtering apparatus
- secrete bile acids
- excretory organ
- covered by Glisson's capsule

- blood supply
  - 75% comes from portal vv
  - 25% comes from hepatic a.

After

St-Pie Notes
AFTER
the Sentence Check-Out

Liver
- functions
  - important storage depot
  - filtering apparatus
  - secrete bile acids
  - excretory organ
  - covered by
    - Glisson's capsule

- blood supply to it
  - 75% comes from portal vv
  - 25% comes from hepatic a.

THE SENTENCE CHECK-OUT PROCEDURE

"This piece of St & Pie is saying that...

...liver functions as an important storage depot   (St → Pie)

...being a filtering apparatus is a liver function   (Pie → St)
...one liver function is to secrete bile acids   (St → Pie)
...the liver functions as an excretory organ   (St → Pie)

indents are okay,
meaning is okay

"This piece of Pie & St is saying that...
...the excretory organ is covered by Glisson's capsule (St→Pie) ——→ incorrect indents give an incorrect meaning

what the Instructor had said was that the liver was covered by Glisson's capsule

"covered by Gl's capsule" is Pie for liver

"This piece of Pie & St is saying that...
...the blood supply is a function of the liver

Incorrect meaning. The indents must be in the wrong place.

(try again) "This piece of Pie & St is saying that the liver sends blood supply to 75% comes from ----

Nope. Doesn't make a sentence. Anyway, doesn't make a sentence without a hassle, like it says on page 50.

(try again) "This piece of Pie & St is saying that the blood supply TO THE LIVER comes from the portal vv

Yup. Okay.
"blood supply"
is Pie for liver (NOT Pie for liver functions)

...75% of the blood supply to liver comes from ---
...25% of the blood supply to liver comes from ---

indents are okay; meaning is okay

Now, don't get up tight about
this check-out business.

You don't have to do it forever.
After a few weeks, your St-Pie
indents just sort of fall into
the right spots automatically.

The only reason for the check out
practice is to get your mind and
ears trained to hear what a
correct St-Pie indent is.

Then, when you get to exam
studying, you know your notes
are okay, and you don't have
to sweat the studying.

This makes you feel
very peaceful.

And this is a good
enough reason to
practice your check-outs.

The other reason is that
if you can't make a sentence,
you won't understand your own notes when you
re-read them

which makes you feel like a fool.

Don't waste your time
playing a busy-busy,
mechanical,
how-pretty-my-notes-look
game with yourself.

because,
when you start to review
for an exam,
if your St-Pie indents are not correct,

you will be in a constant

EYE-MIND CONFLICT

✓ your eye will tell you that something is Pie
for something;
                    and your mind will tell
                    you it isn't.

✓ So, when you're looking over your notes, you'll
keep arguing with yourself about one spot, and
another and another,

                    and what's worse,

                    you'll have to keep trying
                    to remember what you meant
                    when you wrote it down.

                            This is awful, and emotionally
                            exhausting, and results in a
                            strong desire to pitch all the
                            books out the window.

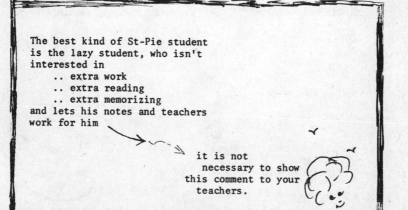

The best kind of St-Pie student
is the lazy student, who isn't
interested in
     .. extra work
     .. extra reading
     .. extra memorizing
and lets his notes and teachers
work for him

                    it is not
                     necessary to show
                    this comment to your
                        teachers.

The difference between stuff that works for
you, and stuff
you have to work on,

is shown on page 47

- the continuous sentences.
- the St-Pie notes

Turn back to that page
and look at both.

I'll wait.

?.... What happened in your mind?... ?

To re-understand the
continuous notes

It was necessary to RE-READ
them ∿∿∿➤ waste of time

To re-understand the
St-Pie notes

It was necessary only to GLANCE
at them ∿∿∿➤ sensible

bird brains ↘

∿∿∿➤if you need to re-read your notes

you don't know how to take notes ∿∿➤and

you are spending too much time

↳ "studying"

St-Pie indenting is a very powerful
tool for Learning Anything.

> The sentence check-out is
> a nuisance, but you get
> a Gift Package with it.

> After you have done
> the check-out.
>
> one hour a day,
> for two weeks,
>
> your Instructors begin
> to talk in St-Pie.

Now I am going to take
two pages to Blow Off Steam.

.. Then we will start St-Pieing stuff from school textbooks.

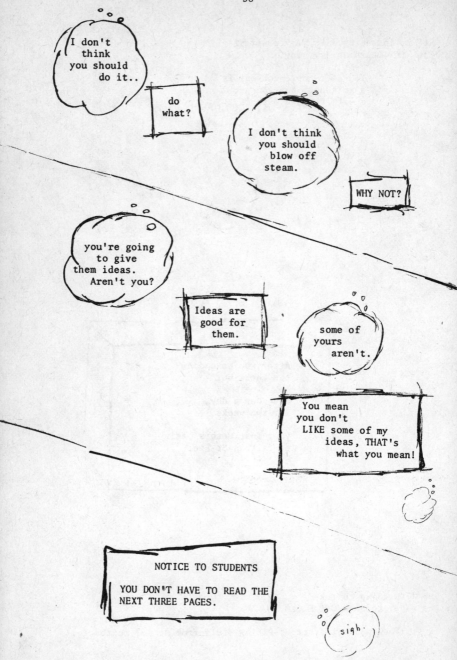

When I was in school, They told me:

Do NOT write down everything that is said in a lecture.

    . Take down only the important ideas.
    . Put in your own words what the Instructor said.
                          (this means " to paraphrase ")
    . Take down the key words.

ULCER FOOD !

How the h--l am I supposed to know
what ideas are important when I
don't even know the subject yet??

And every time I put something in
my own words, my teacher tells me
I missed this essential point or
that essential point. So, okay,
my paraphrases are no good.

So how am I supposed to figure
out ahead of time when I
paraphrase right? and when I do
it wrong????

And I still don't know
what a Key Word is. All I
know is that after I don't
put it in somewhere, some
smart guy tells me what I
was supposed to put down.

My dumb notes used to come out like this: ⟍⟶

Roger Bacon -- inductive reasoning
Henry IV -- Wycliffe and Lolards

Which was no help when I got to
studying for the exam. I couldn't
tell whether Roger Bacon taught it in
his classes, or whether he thought it
was a bad kind of reasoning, or if he
invented it.

And what was it with Henry anyway?
I couldn't remember if Wycliffe and
Lolards influenced Henry; or if
Henry pulled a fast one on them?
or were they opposing clans???

So I had to read the whole
damn textbook over again.

It's all right. They can take their
important Ideas and Key Words and
Paraphrases. In my study system, I
don't need them.

I work backwards. After I've
done the St-Pie techniques, I
can give them all the Key Words
and Important Ideas, and
Paraphrases they want.

Then there were the Generals & the Specifics.

That's another thing they told me about in school.

They said that there were Generals and Specifics,
and in paragraphs you had to have both.

It was a very nice idea.
But it kept getting me in trouble:
when I said something was a specific,
they said no it was a general.

So okay, I wrote in my notebook that it was a general.

Then the next time I said that thing was
a general. But they said no this time
it is a specific.

So okay, after two dozen times I gave up.

But now I have it all figured out

their General is what I call a STATEMENT
and
their Specific is what I call a PIE

AND since any item can be
a Statement or a piece of Pie,
or both (see page 43)...

then an item is a General or
a Specific, depending on
WHERE IT IS in the St-Pie Unit.

Now I can translate my
Statements & Pies into
their generals & specifics
if that's the way they want to talk.

end of blow-off.

rest period

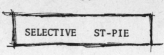

SELECTIVE   ST-PIE

We will now St-Pie from school texbooks,
which I call

SELECTIVE ST-PIE

. because you select the
  Statements and Pies you want
  to use

. and the way you want to put
  them into notes,

. or, if you are a text-underliner,
  the Statements & Pies you want
  to underline for review.

You don't underline
whole paragraphs...
do you???

We will work with

. some stuff that gives you the over-all organization of a chapter

        - Summaries
        - Headings of sections

. two kinds of text content in a chapter

        - one piece where you use almost all the material
        - one piece where there is a lot of repetitious material

. and Visuals, where you don't actually St-Pie at all.

The material in this Section will not always be interesting.

> So don't start out with the idea that you
> are going to enjoy all of it.
>
> I didn't enjoy writing it,
> and no one says you have to like reading it.

> > .. you are not supposed to expect
> > to like everything about a job
> > you have to do.

However, it may help some if you tell yourself that
you're just reading to get an idea of what a
skillful student is doing when he is "studying" from
a textbook.

The first thing you do is see if you can find any SUMMARIES
in the chapter

> - meantime praying that (1) there will be some
> &
> (2) they'll be good ones...

SUMMARIES:

- GIVE THE IMPORTANT STATEMENTS IN THE MATERIAL

    - IF they are good Summaries

- SHOULD BE ST-PIED (usually you should do a complete job of it,

    - if you do this before you read the text
    - you will then have a skeleton of the knowledge in the text
        - the text will be Pie for the summary
        - the text will flesh out the skeleton

- SOME OF THEM ARE NO GOOD

    - if it is a rotten summary, it doesn't help to St-Pie it,
    - but you can't tell if it's rotten until you do St-Pie it.

- CAN BE FOUND

    - at the end of sections within a chapter
    - at the end of the chapter
    - in what is called a REVIEW
    - in what is called an INTRODUCTION

            .. reviews usually summarize preceding material
            .. introductions can summarize preceding material
            or they can summarize the new material
            coming up in the chapter.

                            Kindly do not blame me
                            for the way other people
                            use words.
                                    Thank you

This is a SUMMARY from a Sociology text.*

> Social classes are categories to which people are assigned
> on the basis of prestige. Class systems are found in every
> human society.
> Wealth, family ties, occupation, length of residence, and
> certain personality traits constitute the chief criteria for
> determining social rank. Initially, an individual acquires his
> social rank from a parent, usually his father, but sometimes
> his mother.
> Movement within a social class system may be vertical or
> horizontal. Vertical mobility means movement between classes,
> horizontal mobility means movement within a class. Class

Modern Sociology by Marvin R. Koller and Harold C. Couse, copyright © 1969 by Holt, Rinehart and Winston, Inc. Reprinted by permission of the publisher.

systems may be labeled according to the degree of upward
vertical mobility they permit.

If a system provides little or no opportunity for one to
improve his position, it is called a caste or caste-like
system. If it permits some upward mobility but only on a
selective basis, then it is called an estate system. If
relatively free inter-class movement is permitted, then the
system is called open-class.

The caste system is usually associated with India,
where it was most fully developed. It also existed, however,
in certain Pacific Islands, in parts of the Middle East, and
in tribal Africa. The estate system, a product of medieval
Europe, has been largely discarded. While no completely
open-class system exists in any country, the open-class ideal
has been realized to a considerable extent in America.

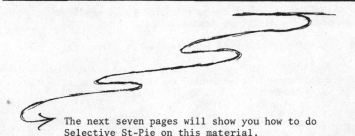

The next seven pages will show you how to do
Selective St-Pie on this material.

There will be a chart in it, and you will
also have to look back-and-forth as the
instructions direct you.

It will not be particularly interesting,
but you will have to suffer through it.

UNFORTUNATELY, these pages are important.

... if you don't read them carefully, you
won't understand how to St-Pie textbook
stuff.

And don't come complaining
to me later that you are
confused.

Instructions for reading the chart on pages 70 & 71

as each thing is
mentioned below, LOCATE
it on the chart or page.

the FIRST COLUMN of the chart
is called

TEXTBOOK MATERIAL

.. this Column contains the text material, the SUMMARY
from a Sociology text, starting on page 66.

.. the material will be → broken up → into small chunks
about one or two sentences each.

The chunks will be separated by horizontal
lines, and numbered ①, ②, etc.

.. the Statement in each chunk will be underlined,
which means that I think of this as "Statement"
in a St-Pie Unit. The Pie for the Statement
will not be underlined.

.. Notice that

✓ sometimes chunks of text material are written with the
Statement first & Pie following,

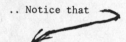 see 1st and 2nd chunks

✓ sometimes the pattern is different: the chunk is written with
some of the Pie first, followed by its Statement...and then by
some more of the Pie,

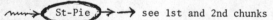 see 3rd chunk

✓ sometimes a whole chunk is a

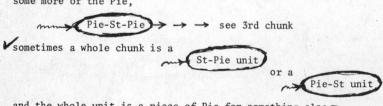

or a

and the whole unit is a piece of Pie for something else

see 5th chunk

---

the SECOND COLUMN of the chart
is called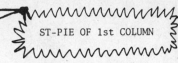

ST-PIE OF 1st COLUMN

.. in this Column are my St-Pie notes for the material
in the First Column.

the THIRD COLUMN of the chart
is called

WHAT I DID

.. this Column explains what I did in making my St-Pie
notes, and my reasons for doing it.

THERE ARE TWO THINGS TO REMEMBER

(1) Whenever you make notes of textbook material, or
St-Pie a Handout given by the Instructor,

you are mentally "selecting" what you think is
important.

Be sure you are not "selecting" only
Statements (because you like them) or
only Pies (because you like them better.)

(2) Whenever you underline in a textbook instead of
making notes,

use one color for the Statements, and a different
color for the Pies.

Be sure you do not Swoosh-Underline.
Students who underline 3,5,7,9, lines
in a text, one after another

are Swoosh-Underliners. They are
unconsciously muttering to themselves, "This feels important...
swoosh...I'll come back to it when
I...swoosh...have time."

You never have time.

...I trust you followed the Instructions at the top of page 68 ??

TEXTBOOK MATERIAL	ST-PIE OF 1st COLUMN	WHAT I DID
(1) Social classes are categories to which people are assigned on the basis of prestige.	Social classes - categories to which people assigned - basis = prestige	St-Pied it with indents
(2) Class systems are found in every human society.	Class systems - found in every human society	St-Pied it with indents

(3) Wealth, family ties, occupation length of residence, and certain personality traits constitute the chief criteria for determining social rank.
 	
Initially, an individual acquires his social rank from a parent, usually his father, but sometimes his mother.
	Social rank
	- criteria for determining it
	  - wealth
	  - family ties
	  - occupation
	  - etc.
	- acquired by individual
	  - initially from parent
	  - usually father
		I saw that SOCIAL RANK was a Statement in both sentences, so I "selected" it out as the single Statement for all the Pie in both sentences.
		
		I do this whenever I find a COMMON STATEMENT, or a REPEAT STATEMENT, in different places of the text material.

(4) Movement within a Social class system may be vertical or horizontal. Vertical mobility means movement between classes; horizontal mobility means movement within a class.	Social Class systems
	- movement within them
	  - vertical mobility = mvmnt
	    \between classes
	  - horizontal mobility = mvmnt
	    \within a class
	- labeled by degree of VERTICAL
	    \mobility permitted
		I saw that SOCIAL CLASS SYSTEM and CLASS SYSTEMS (see chunk 2) mean the same thing in these sentences; just different phrases.
		
		Each had Pie for it, so I "selected" out SOCIAL CLASS SYSTEMS as the single Statement for all the Pies in both sentences.

⑤ If a system provides little or no opportunity for one to improve his position, it is called a caste or caste-like system.

(labeled by degree of...)
- caste (or caste-like) systems
- opportunity to improve = none
  / or little

...see page 109 for use of parentheses here.

Within the sentence itself, the order is Pie→St. I St-Pied it.

The whole sentence is Pie for "labeled by..." in chunk 4. So I make this whole St-Pie Unit a piece of Pie for "labeled by..."

⑥ If it permits some upward mobility, but only on a selective basis, then it is called an estate system.

- estate system
  - some upward mobility
  - on selective basis

This sentence is, again, a piece of Pie for "labeled by..." as in chunk 5.

⑦ If it permits relatively free inter-class movement, then the system is called open-class.

- open class system
  - free inter-class mvment

... same as above...

⑧ The caste system is usually associated with India, where it was most fully developed. It also existed, however, in certain Pacific Islands, in parts of the Middle East, and in tribal Africa.

- caste system
  - India = most developed
  - some Pacific Islands
  - parts of Middle East
  - tribal Africa

Here the author starts again on CASTE-SYSTEM, chunk 5...giving us more Pie for the common Statement. So, do this

St-Pie chunk 8, draw a bracket around it. Draw an arrow to show it is Pie for "caste (or caste-like) system" in chunk 5. (Also see pages 110 & 111 for cut-&-paste idea)

I do the same with the rest of the textbook material (page 67)
as I did with chunk 8 (page 71).

I now have correct St-Pie Units,
which state exactly what the book said.

For some people, this is enough.

But, different people have

different kinds of minds, and
my kind of mind likes to take
in what the whole thing is about
in sort of a quick glance...

So I usually St-Pie the first two levels of the
indents to see what I've got:

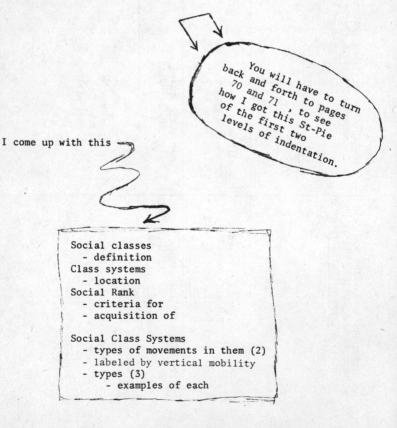

You will have to turn
back and forth to pages
70 and 71 , to see
how I got this St-Pie
of the first two
levels of indentation.

I come up with this

Social classes
   - definition
Class systems
   - location
Social Rank
   - criteria for
   - acquisition of

Social Class Systems
   - types of movements in them (2)
   - labeled by vertical mobility
   - types (3)
      - examples of each

I now have a fuzz-area:

> I am not sure of the
> difference between
> CLASS SYSTEMS and
>   SOCIAL CLASS SYSTEMS.

I look at the Pie under each
of these headings (Statements).

From the Pie, I figure out
that the book is using both
things to mean the same thing.

I choose one, and scribble
all the Pies under it.

I have another fuzz-area.

> I am not sure of the
> difference between
> SOCIAL CLASS and
>   SOCIAL RANK....

I look at the Pie under
each of them.

The book is using both
word clumps to mean
the same thing.

I choose one, and scribble
all the Pies under it.

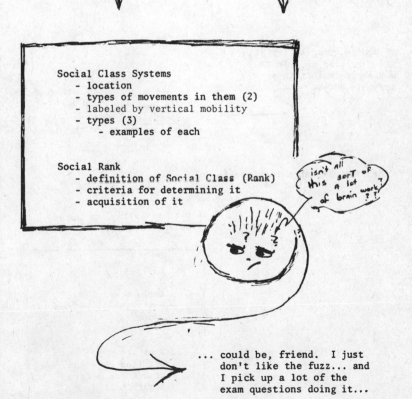

Social Class Systems
- location
- types of movements in them (2)
- labeled by vertical mobility
- types (3)
    - examples of each

Social Rank
- definition of Social Class (Rank)
- criteria for determining it
- acquisition of it

isn't all this sort of a lot of brain work??

... could be, friend. I just
don't like the fuzz... and
I pick up a lot of the
exam questions doing it...

Besides, by the time I've fooled around
with the stuff this way, I've been over
it a couple of times,

and by the time I've got most of the kinks
worked out

        it's half-way memorized.

        Comes exam time, I turn
        the St-Pies into questions;
        check out what I still
        remember, memorize the rest,

                and I'm home free and out to a
                ball game that's more fun than
                sitting with a textbook.

If you're going to try it,
you should be certain to
use abbreviations in your
scribble notes.

          - I <u>scribble</u> it.
          - I <u>abbreviate</u> everything in it.
          - I <u>advise</u> you to do the same.

Otherwise, it takes too long to do.

        If I had been abbreviating, my notes
        would have looked like this

```
Soc Cl  sys
   - loc
   - types mvmnts (2)
   - basis labelling 'em
   - types (3)
      - ex each

Soc Rank
   - def (soc cl = soc rank)
   - criter for determ
   - acquisit of
```

It's no more work than learning how
to swim, or ride a bike -- if you
practice for two weeks you can get
practically all your lectures like
this in ten minutes

   and pull a textbook chapter
together in fifteen or twenty
minutes...

      and THEN you can rattle off
      what the chapter or
      lecture was talking about

         like this

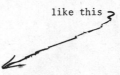

TEACHER: "Mr. Jones, what did you think of the chapter that
          was assigned for today?"

STUDENT: "I thought the chapter presented the fundamentals of
          class systems quite clearly. It discussed social
          class systems and social rank. Under social class
          systems, the author discussed where they are found,
          the two types of movements that occur in them, and
          the basis or method by which they are labeled --the
          degree of vertical mobility was his criteria for the
          three types of social class systems he discussed.

          The author defined the term 'social rank' as the
          person's social class within a system, gave several
          criteria for how one's class or rank is determined,
          and stated how a person acquired his class or rank."

How would you like to be able to rattle off
a nice learned-sounding bunch of words like
that?

      How do you think the guys and gals who
      impress their teachers -- AND impress
      you, too -- do it???

         Like that. Just like that.

Rest period...

    for absorbing the
information up to here.

← sleeping
  author

Take a break for a day
or two

then go back and re-do
pages 70 through 74

they are very
important.

ABOUT HEADINGS IN CHAPTERS:

. The Headings of chapter sections
        . are supposed to be "break-up points", like topics
        . they may be in dark print (called "bold face")
                    or in color
                    or in italics
                    or etceteras

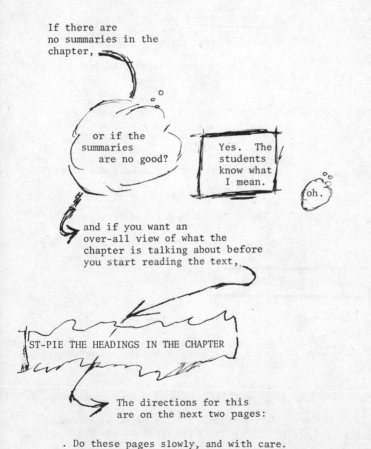

If there are
no summaries in the
chapter,

or if the
summaries
    are no good?

Yes. The
students
know what
I mean.

oh.

and if you want an
over-all view of what the
chapter is talking about before
you start reading the text,

ST-PIE THE HEADINGS IN THE CHAPTER

The directions for this
are on the next two pages:

. Do these pages slowly, and with care.
. No one is telling you to enjoy it. Just do it.

They are very
stuffed-with-information pages.

78

A list of section headings from a textbook chapter:*

1 What is meant by Social Class

2 The basis of Social Class Systems
3   vary from society to society

4 Class is determined by a combination
5   of factors

6 Two kinds of Social Mobility

7 Class Systems : three kinds

8 Caste systems are very rigid

9 The estate system flourished during
10   the Middle Ages

11 Open-class systems provide many
12   avenues for advancement

13 Open-class system prevails in the
14   United States

15 Social mobility in the United States

16 Stratification affects life chances

17 The Communist myth of a classless
18   society

HOW TO ST-PIE THESE HEADINGS

(1) Mark with   circles / boxes / color / lines / all
     the
         ➘ REPEAT WORDS in the headings.
     and ➙ WORDS you feel or think have the SAME MEANING.

(2) Start your St-Pie scribble notes (abbreviate as on p.74)

     . write down the Headings you think might be Statements.
          Statements are usually Repeat or New Topic words.

     . between each Statement, leave an inch or so to be
          filled in later with the Headings that are Pies.

*Modern Sociology by Marvin R. Koller and Harold C. Couse, copyright © 1969 by Holt,
Rinehart and Winston, Inc. Reprinted by permission of the publisher.

(3) From the Headings on page 78, you get this set of scribbles

> Social class / class
>
> Social class Systems / class systems
>
> Social mobility
>
> Open class / classless

Leave an inch between the Statements.

(4) To make up the St-Pie units ──▶ fill in with the rest of the Headings, which are probably Pies for the above Sts. AND

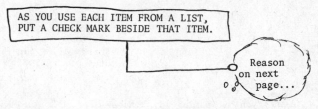

> AS YOU USE EACH ITEM FROM A LIST, PUT A CHECK MARK BESIDE THAT ITEM.

Reason on next page...

I have numbered the items instead of check-marking, so you can follow what I did when I went from the list of section Headings (page 78) to this

> a St-Pie of the section headings

1,4	Social Class
1	- meaning of
4,5	- factors which determine it
2,7	Social Class Systems
2,3	- basis for them vary with diff. societies
7	- kinds of (3)
8	- caste system = rigid
9,10	- estate system = Middle Ages
11,13,14	- open-class = U.S.A.
12	- avenues for advancement
6	- social mobility in
6	- kinds (types) = 2
15	- in U.S.A.

16	Stratification affects life chances
17,18	Communist myth of a classless society

left-over items

TRICKS OF THE TRADE OF STUDYING:

✓ - The reason for checking off items
as you use them
is to keep your mind peaceful.

If you check off items as you go,
you can quit studying at
any time, and come back to it,
and know where you left off.

If you <u>don't</u> check off as you go,
even while you are working,
your mind will skitter back and
forth like a mouse, trying to
see did I use this before? did I
use that? did I put that down
in three places????

✓ - When you are making any kind of St-Pie,
add in words as necessary to make
a sensible, readable St-Pie for
yourself...

... for example, add in words like
. types
. reasons
. causes
. examples
. etceteras

✓ - When you have "left-over items" as I
did on page 79

write them at the bottom of your scribble notes

Left-overs are the pieces which will not fit
easily into St-Pie Units.

Don't hassle them.

And don't let them hassle you.
You're not after a perfect
Over-All Organization (OAO)
of the material,

That's
me.

a general over-view
is all you need.

How about you St-Pieing this next stuff?

.. St-Pie it
.. then check it with my St-Pie at the bottom
   of this page, upsidedown

.. start out with →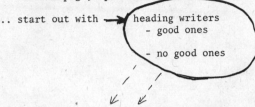

Some heading-writers are really good. Their stuff can be St-Pied into an over-all organization of the chapter, just as a good summary can. But some heading writers are no good. Watch out for this. When you get through reading their section headings, you can end up more confused than if you hadn't looked at the headings at all. If this happens, don't let it throw you...have some respect for yourself. It is not always your fault when you don't understand something. Most of the time it is; but not all the time.

Keep in your head these very important points: a text-book is not a Sacred Cow, chapter headings do not always make sense, writers are not always clear (not even me), and you are not always a dumb reader.

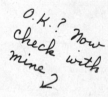

not use of the marker.

Heading-writers
    - good = some
    - St-Pie ← good organization of chapter
    - same as good summary-writer
    - no good = some
    - leave you confused
    - not always your fault
Books — important points
    - textbooks = not sacred
    - Headings = not always sensible
    - writers = " " clear
    - student = " " dumb reader

If there's no Summary
and if the heading-writer was a dope,

you might have to Selective St-Pie
the text itself. So we'll do that next.

ADVICE

it is usually wise to read over the
inside of a chapter,

even if you've already got a good idea
of the material from the Summary-St-Pie
or the Headings-St-Pie.

I have
personally
passed three courses
just doing Summaries..
... but I did use
all the techniques...
not just the
St-Pie one.

DON'T TELL
THEM THAT !

You KNOW the real
understanding comes
from reading the
chapter afterwards

I didn't tell them NOT to
read the chapter !
I just said if they
know how to do it, they
can PASS a course
without reading too much
in the books...

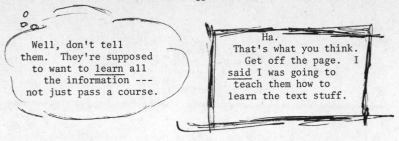

Well, don't tell them. They're supposed to want to <u>learn</u> all the information --- not just pass a course.

Ha.
That's what you think. Get off the page. I said I was going to teach them how to learn the text stuff.

<u>THE TEXT STUFF</u>

..this is the first kind of text content where you use almost all of the material given.

This is the text material

A study of the nature and patterns of culture is valuable because it permits one to make objective comparisons between different ways of life. A student who understands cultural diversity is in a good position to understand his own culture as well as the cultures of other peoples. He is able to view differences in human behavior in perspective because he realizes that men in different situations have adopted alternate means of meeting their needs. To be sure, he may prefer the solutions evolved by his own society to those offered by others. But if he learned anything at all from his studies, he will...etc.

The next two pages is a CHART of this material.
In the chart

I indented the sentences as if they were Statements & Pies.

.. this makes me a very nice person, because it is a damn nuisance

for me to do it this way.

TEXT MATERIAL

A study of the nature and patterns of culture is valuable

- because

  - it permits one to make objective comparisons between different ways of life.

- A student who understands cultural diversity is in a good position to understand

  - his own culture as well as the cultures of other peoples.

  - He is able to view differences in human behavior in perspective because he realizes that men in different situations have adopted alternate means of meeting their needs.

  - To be sure, he may prefer the solutions evolved by his own society to those offered by others.

  - But if he learned anything at all from his studies, he will avoid the error of condemning a cultural trait simply because it is unfamiliar.

ST-PIE OF TEXT MATERIAL

Study of { nature & patterns } of culture = VALUABLE

- because

  - permits objective comparison between diff. cultures

  - student can understand
    - other cultures & own
    - diff. situations require diff. solutions
    - so cultures are different
    - he may prefer solutions of own culture
  - student won't condemn people with diff. cultural traits
    - because of unfamiliarity with them

Ethnocentrism

- human tendency to judge other cultures in \ terms of similarity to our own
- undue pride in familiar ways of life
  - undervalue different   "   "
- all societies have it
  - varying degrees
  - favor own culture above others
- mirrored in self-chosen names
  - "Chung Kuo" means "Central land"
  - Greeks vs. "barbarian" non-Greeks
- DANGEROUS in small world of today
  - undue pride in own culture = conflict with others
  - not dangerous when societies are isolated
    - think of self as "best" = okay

> The first Pie under Ethnocentrism is the definition of the word. Always write out Defs. fully.

The human tendency to judge other cultures in terms of how similar they are to one's own culture is known as ethnocentrism.

- Ethnocentrism consists in taking undue pride in familiar ways of life
  - while undervaluing those which differ.
- All societies are, to varying degrees, ethnocentric;
  - all tend to favor their own cultures above others.
- Often, ethnocentric feelings are mirrored in the names societies coin for themselves.
  - For example, the Chinese name for China is "Chung Kuo" which means "Central land".
  - The Greeks had the same idea when they reserved the term "civilized" for themselves, and referred to non-Greeks as "barbarians".

So long as societies remain isolated, ethnocentrism is not necessarily harmful.

- Under such conditions each person can think of his culture as the finest, without antagonizing other peoples.

- In our small world, however, undue pride in one's culture can be a source of conflict.

- It is this potential effect of ethnocentrism that renders it dangerous.

After the text material is St-Pied,
it is easier to "take-in" what it's
talking about,

> and figure out how the two main Statements
> link up: <u>The study of cultures is valuable</u>
> and <u>Ethnocentrism</u>.

If I just read the text material, without making notes on it,
I have to hold all the words and ideas in my head while I
examine them. Sometimes this is easy, sometimes it isn't. With
the St-Pie notes I can examine the ideas at my leisure. Here
the author is saying

. the study of cultures is valuable for three reasons

. doing objective comparisons of cultures
. helping person understand how different cultures
\ came about
. keeping person from condemning other cultures

. Ethnocentrism is the cause of condemning other cultures

. Ethnocentrism is undue "self-pride" in one's own
\ culture
. Ethnocentrism is dangerous in today's small world;
it causes conflicts between countries.

(The author might be implying -- he hasn't <u>said</u> it -- that
if more people studied various cultures, then there might
not be so much Ethnocentrism in the world.)

SELECTIVE ST-PIE started
on page 64.

> You can see now that Selective St-Pie has
> two kinds of meanings...and two kinds of
> freedoms .

(1) You can select from the text what to put into your
notes.

(2) You can select the way you St-Pie it. If the text
reads from Pie → St → Pie, you can make your notes
St → Pie. If the text scatters the Pies and Sts
all over the place, you can get them together and
clump them where you wish.

Now we will go on to
another kind of text material..

.. this is the second kind of text material
.. where there is a lot of repetitious material

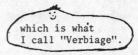
which is what
I call "Verbiage".

Get clearly in your mind the
fact that when most people
write or talk,

- they repeat themselves
- " use more words than necessary
- " use different words for the same things.

I don't know exactly why,
but I think it comes because

. maybe they feel that using a lot of different
words gives their writing "style"

.& they don't realize that
this confuses the reader?

. or maybe they feel that when they're talking
they sound smarter if they sling around a lot
of words?...it does show how many ways they
can say the same thing.

. or it could be they have been told it is a
Good Thing to have a Large Vocabulary?

. You might as well accept the
fact that schools are filled
with Large Vocabulary people
and books.

Now what I'd like you to try
is to cover up my St-Pie notes
of the text material on the next two pages,

and try St-Pieing the text yourself.

It won't come out the same as mine, and it isn't supposed to. Everyone St-Pies differently.

I have smudged over certain parts of the text to show that I consider them Verbiage.

Read it and see if you agree or not. If not, we can fight. I say it's Verbiage.

THE SELECTIVE ST-PIE NOTES

Book shows how Archaeology
- interprets the past
- reconstructs past

Archaeology
- History of
  - early development
  - chronology
  - site surveys
  - excavations

THE TEXT MATERIAL

~~This~~ book on archaeology ~~deals with the complexity and vastness of man's past~~ in a way that the ~~student can both under-~~ ~~stand and enjoy. It examines all aspects~~ ~~of archaeology rather than concentrating~~ ~~on one particular part of the field.~~ This thorough ~~approach~~ allows the student ~~to~~ ~~grasp the enormous periods of time with~~ ~~which archaeology deals, as well as~~ to perceive the many ways it interprets and reconstructs the past.

The book treats the history, the methodology, and the theory of archaeology. ~~It is~~ ~~divided into three sections:~~ part one deals with archaeology's early development, chronology, and with site survey and excavations; part two focuses on the research methods and field techniques archaeologists use to analyze and describe

- Methodology
  - research methods
  - field techniques
- USES
  - analyze & describe
    - prehistoric
    - economies
    - artifacts

- Theories
  - development of explanations of Past
  - earliest = 1970's
  - Old World
  - New World

- Examples from
  - all parts of world
  - all time periods

Remember

prehistoric economies and artifacts; part three traces the development of explanations of the past from the earliest times to the 1970's, including Old and New World theories of archaeology. By breaking down this vast subject into distinct parts, the book provides a comprehensive summary for those students who have not yet encountered the prehistoric past.

This is a wide-ranging and thought provoking study, discussing all areas of archaeology, in all parts of the world and all time periods. The many interesting examples are drawn from Siberia, Africa, Asia, Europe, North and Central America, Australia and New Zealand. There is also greater discussion of the New World approach to archaeology. All of these features help the student to comprehend archaeology's intellectual framework and makes him aware of the field's latest advances.

How do our notes compare?

The Verbiage Problem is always going to crop up.
You can't do anything about THAT,

but after St-Pieing becomes automatic
for you,

you don't have to be impressed
with anyone's verbiage.

and you don't have to feel
hopeless when you meet it in
a book.

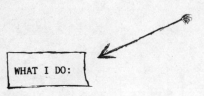

WHAT I DO:

.. I read something like that material on pages 88 & 89
in a very fast hurry

.. then I immediately start to make St-Pie scribble
notes.

.. When I've got the notes in pretty good shape
  - if they're too messy to read I copy them first
  - if they're readable, I paste them into my
    notebook just as they are.

THEN, I never look

at that piece

of the book again.

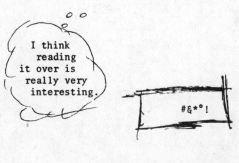

SCRIBBLE-NOTES MECHANICS

** Keep plenty of scratch paper beside you when
you start to St-Pie text material....You want to be able
to scribble, abbreviate, scratch up the sheet of notes as
you gradually learn what the material is telling you.

If you have nice, clean, beautiful, expensive paper,
and if you make nice, beautiful neat notes

the neatness will get in your way. You will not be
able to make yourself scratch-up the paper, and shift
and change the notes until the material is organized.

** You also need to work on only one side of the paper, so
that you can lay out the sheets and look at all the notes
at one time.

If you want to save money and the ecology: when you
have finished with one side of the paper, mark a large X
through it. Use the other side in your next St-Pie
organizing session.

That's all for the moment
on Textbook St-Pieing.

The next stuff is about
lecture St-Pieing,

so this would be a good
stopping point for some
                        other
                              kind
                                  of
                                      recreation.

NOTEBOOK INFORMATION

. you can use a spiral bound notebook

. or a looseleaf notebook

. or a spiral bound with looseleaf holes

BUT

. Only use <u>one</u> side of the notebook
. The other side is for
    . adding in new material on the same topic
    . paste-in space for diagrams & stuff from Handouts
    . fix-ups of your own St-Pie lecture notes

all of which will be
explained in the
Things-that-bother-you
section, page 102

Small size notebooks cause cramps of the mind
for most people. I use 8½ by 11 size.

Experiment.

Experiment.

THIS SECTION IS ABOUT

- TAKING NOTES IN A LECTURE

.. Many people say that
there is only one way
to take notes. This
is a lie.

✓ you use SELECTIVE ST-PIE   ✓ you use RECORDING ST-PIE

| When you are taking notes on something you are READING. |

| When you are taking notes on something you are HEARING like a LECTURE, or a discussion. |

| Please do not mix them up. |

The difference between
the two techniques is
a TIME FACTOR.

When you are reading something,
you have Time.
You can hunt around in the
paragraphs and pick out the
St-Pies you want to put
together.

BUT...when you are in a lecture,
or in a class discussion,
there's no Time for waiting
around and selecting out St-Pies.

By the time you have figured out
what one part was about, the
Instructor is already into a new
topic....

... you have missed the start
of the new topic because you were
making notes on the old topic..
..you're lost? ⌒⌒⌒ since there's
no use taking down "nonsense" words...
the mind-wandering and day-dreaming
during the lecture...begins...

RECORDING ST-PIE TECHNIQUE:

Take down every damn thing you can get down during a lecture.

- the first trick is to RECORD EXACTLY what the Instructor says, <u>as he is saying it.</u>

    . even if you think you don't understand it, don't just sit there like a goop waiting for it all to be clear,

    . get everything down. Information should go from the ear, to the pencil, to the paper immediately.

    . some pieces you'll hear in St-Pie Units. Write them down that way,

    . the rest, take down any which way it's easiest.

- the second trick is to put the whole lecture into St-Pie Units THAT SAME DAY.

    . if you do it the same day, you'll be able to recall a lot of stuff you didn't get into the notes.

        . add this recall-stuff to your notes.

    . there will be parts, at first, you won't be able to St-Pie. Put a question mark beside these parts and ask a friend what the Instructor meant...so you find out what items you left out.

Remember, after a few weeks, the Instructor talks more and more in St-Pie Units,

you have less and less "homework" to do on your notes, and

if you like to read, you can read a book. Some people like to read.

There are certain THINGS that cause
problems when you are taking notes
in lecture.

. Sometimes
these THINGS occur because of the time
factor (see page 94).

. Other times
they occur because the lecturer may be
constantly changing his
St-Pie patterns.

St ⟶ Pie
Pie ⟶ St
etc...

For example:

He may start out talking
about animal G, and tell
you what species it is.

Then he may discuss various
things about animals K & Z.

Then he may return to animal G
and talk about its living habits,

then to animal Z's characteristics

then to animal G's characteristics

etc...

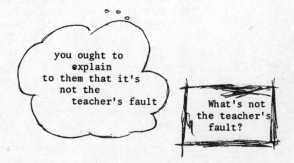

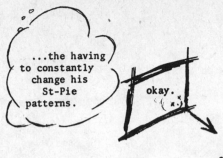

...the having to constantly change his St-Pie patterns.

okay.

It's not the teacher's fault the teacher has to keep changing his organization St-Pie patterns.

sigh.

Now, obviously, during a lecture you can't keep rushing back and forth all over your notes, trying to put all the Pies for animal K in one place.

Lecture note-taking should be a quiet and peaceful interlude in your day.

It should not be disrupted by THINGS.

Now, the best way to deal with a THING

is

to

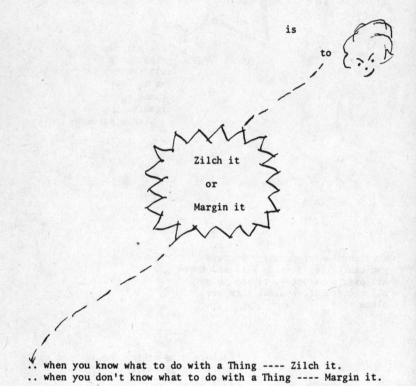

Zilch it

or

Margin it

.. when you know what to do with a Thing ---- Zilch it.
.. when you don't know what to do with a Thing ---- Margin it.

This is the basic technique
for dealing with most of the
Things-that-bother-you
in a lecture.

EXAMPLE OF A ZILCH-IT

The lecturer is babbling along & you've been St-Pieing fine, and then he says:

> "The Red dog was the daughter of the
> Yellow dog who had 4 pups, 3 brown, one
> of which was spotted, and one red."

Well -- who had the 4 pups? The daughter, or the Yellow...??

This causes St-Pie confusion. Therefore, use a Zilch

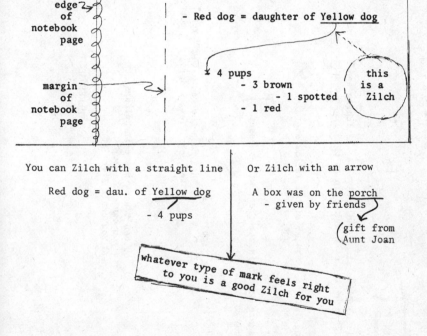

You can Zilch with a straight line   Or Zilch with an arrow

Red dog = dau. of <u>Yellow dog</u>   A box was on the <u>porch</u>
                - 4 pups   - given by friends)

                                            (gift from
                                            (Aunt Joan

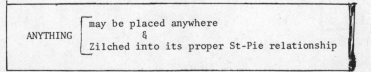

whatever type of mark feels right to you is a good Zilch for you

A Zilch is used
    - to link items together
    - to Pie one piece of a Statement or item
    - to give you freedom of the page

ANYTHING [may be placed anywhere
         &
         Zilched into its proper St-Pie relationship

EXAMPLE OF A MARGIN-IT

The lecturer is babbling along and you've been Zilching and St-Pieing at a great rate. Then he suddenly throws in an un-Zilchable sentence:

"The Red dog was the daughter of the Yellow dog who had 4 pups, 3 brown, one of which was spotted, and one red."

" Such dogs are common in the great wildernesses."

Your problem is:

What does the "such dogs" refer to?? Red dogs, Yellow dogs, or spotted Brown dogs??

. You don't know where it belongs,
. so you can't St-Pie it
. and you can't Zilch-it.

THEREFORE

you MARGIN-IT

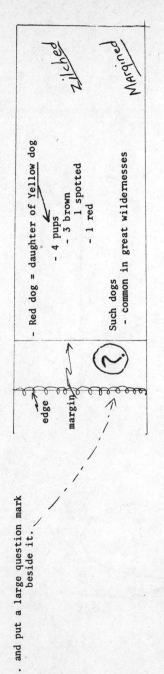

. and put a large question mark
  beside it.

. The question mark is put in the margin so you don't
have to keep "remembering" all the things you didn't
understand at the time.

  To carry such rememberings in your
  head overloads the circuits of the
  mind. Causes fuzz. Mental cruelty.

. That evening the Student asked a friend what
"such dogs" referred to, and was told that
"such dogs" referred to the "Red dogs"

  The student then
  - Zilched the two items together
  - crossed out the question mark

We are now going to do a section on

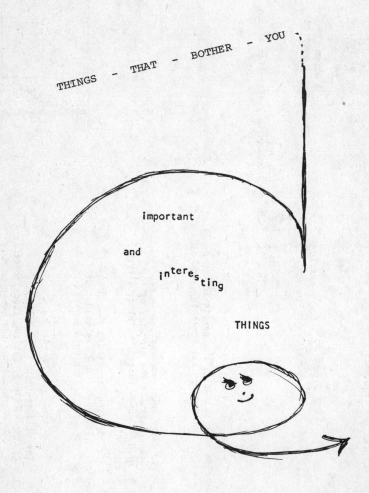

THINGS - THAT - BOTHER - YOU

important

and

interesting

THINGS

THING # 1

  .. What do I do when I get Pie for both parts of
     a Statement ?

> The lecturer says : " apples make good
> eating because they satisfy, nourish,
> and also please the eye. As a fruit
> improved by man, they provide Vitamin C
> and grit for the teeth."

SOLUTION

.. Zilch both sets of Pie

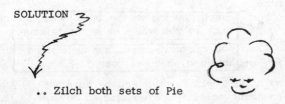

Apples make good eating
    – satisfy
    – nourish
    – please the eye

– fruit
  – improved by man
  – provide { Vitamin C
           grit for teeth

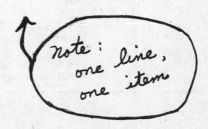

note : one line,
one item

THING #2

.. Where do I write the Pie for a Diagram of something?

.. that's easy ↘
                    put the Pie anywhere, and use a
                    Sideways Zilch.

Example: The lecturer speaks ↙

" Now then, as you all know, Thyroxin has a very
interesting structure..

much drawing on the board with his
back to you while he keeps talking

"...this structure as
you can see...

you can neither see nor understand
anything, but you keep St-Pieing

"...has two Phenyl groups which are joined by an ether
bond, and has an amino acid, which we studied several
weeks ago. Of particular importance in this Thyroxin is
the fact that it has four Iodine molecules."

You St-P and Zilch (as it suits your mind)

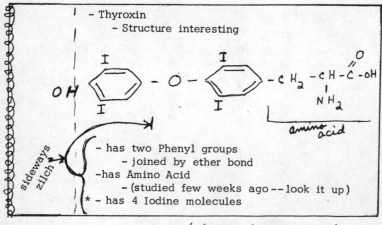

(* means important item)

THING # 3

  .. What do I do when I have the <u>same</u> Pie for two items in a Statement ?

    <u>Example:</u>

        " Kicking the yellow dog and the black cat will give you very sick animals. "

ANSWER

  .. Bracket the two items on both sides and Pie as usual.

    <u>Example:</u>

$$- \text{Kick} \begin{bmatrix} \text{yellow dog} \\ \& \\ \text{black cat} \end{bmatrix}$$

      - gives sick animals

Note:

    If you had no brackets, like this

      - Kicking   yellow dog
                    &
              black cat
                    - gives sick animals

    Or one bracket, like this

$$\text{Kicking} \left\{ \begin{array}{l} \text{yellow dog} \\ \& \\ \text{black cat} \\ \text{- gives sick animals} \end{array} \right.$$

...your Eye would be saying to your Mind : that if you kick the dog and the cat, only the cat gets sick.

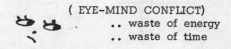

            (EYE-MIND CONFLICT)
               .. waste of energy
               .. waste of time

THING #4

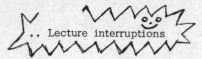

.. Lecture interruptions

1) The lecturer is babbling along and someone
   interrupts with a question.

2) The lecturer suddenly interrupts himself and says,
   "Oh, by the way, I forgot to mention yesterday
   that the...

   ⮕ Where does yesterday's left-over go?

3) You suddenly get a Brilliant Idea. It may be related
   to this lecture, or it may not be -- but it is definitely
   a Brilliant Idea.

   ⮕ How to keep it from being drowned
     by the lecturer's outpouring of verbiage?

SOLUTION

   For all interruptions
   - { margin / bracket } them

   - continue with St-P as if they had not happened

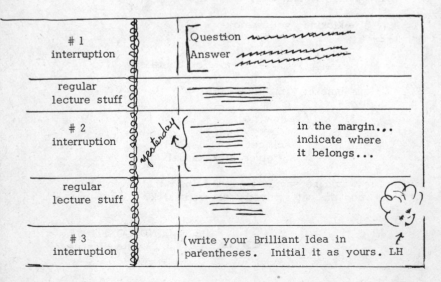

THING # 5	ANSWER
.. What do I do when the St-Pie indents are running off the page?	.. Squnch it up at the right-hand side of page AND .. Use a line to show the squnch-up is NOT a Pie.

EXAMPLE OF

a slanted-line squnch-up

TV changing rapidly
- fast changing technology
- need for high-paid TV commercial
  writers creating new stuff

same material WITHOUT a squnch-up

TV changing rapidly
- fast changing technology
- need for high-paid TV commercial
  writers creating new stuff

..to your EYE and to your MIND this material says that TV is changing rapidly because of a fast changing technology, and TV changes create a need for TV commercial writers.

...to your EYE, in spite of the little indent dashes, this material is saying to your MIND: that TV changes rapidly because of a fast changing technology, the need for the TV commercials, and the writers who are creating new stuff

This is incorrect data. In three weeks time, you might be able to untangle it IF you can still remember the lecture.

Any kind of a line will do for a squnch-up this is a box-type line

- Secretion of NH_4 may rise to 600 meg/day

THING # 6

  .. How come I get a lot of squnch-ups in my notes?

Reason

  # (1) You may be allowing too much space for your
           Pie indenting.

                  A piece of Pie should be indented
                  about 1/2 or 3/4 inches under its St.

                                 OK

not good _____

                _____

Reason

  # (2) You are not doing St-P correctly, because

          .. you have not followed the rule of
             one line, one item

          .. you are not zilching enough

** *usual reason*   {   .. you have not done the required half an hour
              each day, re-writing your messy and incorrect
              notes into correct St-P form

Solution for   }   .. do the required homework
excessive squnch-ups   &
                      .. re-write squnch-ups into
                         St-P form

Information (useful): when you
are taking correct St-Pie notes,   — *but you don't have to take St-Pie notes!*
only one or two squnch-ups occur

THING # 7

.. you go to the next page in your notebook -- where do you start writing your notes ? ?

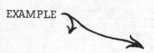

.. At the margin of the new page.
    .. whether the item is a St or is Pie -- margin it and
    .. scribble above the item, in parentheses, what the item is talking about.

EXAMPLE

notebook page

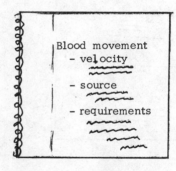

new notebook page

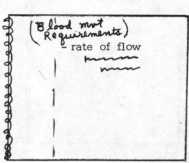

... the next Technique will show you how to relate the St-Pie units to each other

        But first you have to have the St-Pie units,

......so start each new page AT the margin. Thank you.

THING # 8

. the Slot-ins

               for textbooks & Handouts by lecturer

THE PROCEDURE

. St-Pie the lecture   use Recording St-Pie, please (page 94)

- notebook -

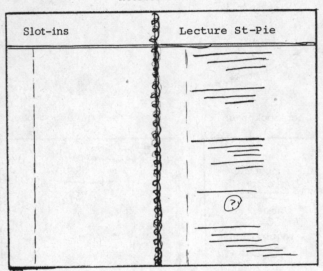

..... Skim the text or handout for any NEW stuff
     you didn't get in lecture.

                            Ignore everything
     in the text or handout that is already in your
     notes.

.. on the page OPPOSITE to your St-P notes,
   St-P the new material

   **(This is why you take notes on only
   one side of the page.)**

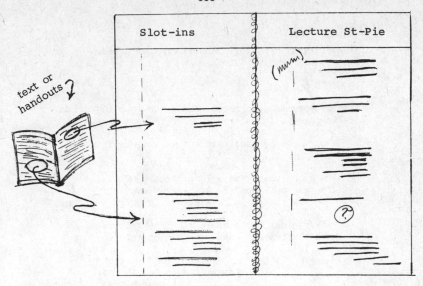

...and ARROW IT into its place in the St-Pie lecture notes.

.....Make the heads of the arrows MEET, so you know what goes with what → *like this* →

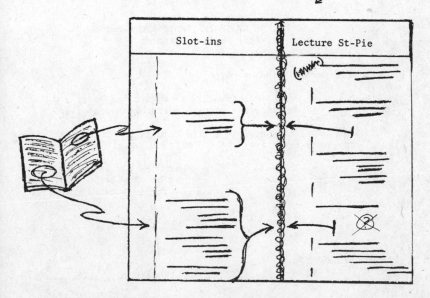

THING # 9

... the Fix-Ups, used for homework on your notes.

THE PROBLEM

Some of your lecture notes didn't come out in correct St-Pie relationships, or

some of them came out in run-on sentences.

In either case, this is perfectly okay.
You are not supposed to "force" yourself
to take things in St-Pie.

After class, you should take the incorrects
and the run-ons, and fix them up into correct
St-Pie.

This practice does two things:
- it corrects your notes
- it corrects your note-taking hang-ups

HOW TO DO THE FIX-UPS

. On the page OPPOSITE your lecture St-Pie notes,
re-write the small pieces that are incorrect or
run-ons.

DO NOT RE-WRITE THE WHOLE LECTURE *!$#&¢%+?!!
. that would be stupid
. and time-wasting

. Slot-in the fixed-up notes

(I usually do the fix-ups on scratch paper and
then paste it into the notebook as a slot-in.)

. with color crayon, draw a line through the notes that
have been re-written

so that when you are ready to
review for exams, you will not
be reading duplicated material.

DIAGRAM OF NOTEBOOK PAGES ⟶

next page, please ⟶

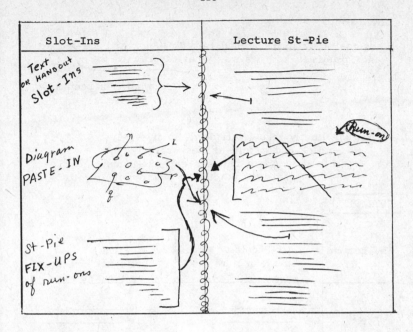

If you need more space for a particular notebook page:

   ✔ tape more paper to the Slot-in page
   ✔ fold this extra paper into the notebook

THE PROCEDURE you want to follow is this

      . do fix-ups of your lecture notes
      . do slot-ins from texts & handouts as necessary
      . paste-in laboratory or other diagrams as relevant

Now everything on any given topic is altogether in one
place. There is no Verbiage, because you have eliminated
this as you selected what was new and what wasn't from
texts, handouts, laboratory.

     At exam-preparation time, you
     can now leave your Handouts in
     their pile, and your textbooks on
     their shelves,
       and study from your single notebook.

it makes you feel frightfully superior

THING # 10

.. the instructor jumps around from St→Pie, and Pie→St, and sometimes both ways. What to do with it?

Do what has been said:

.. just quietly take it all down as it is given
- zilch and margin as necessary
- leave a space between each St-P unit
- the same day, put the St where you like it

EXAMPLE

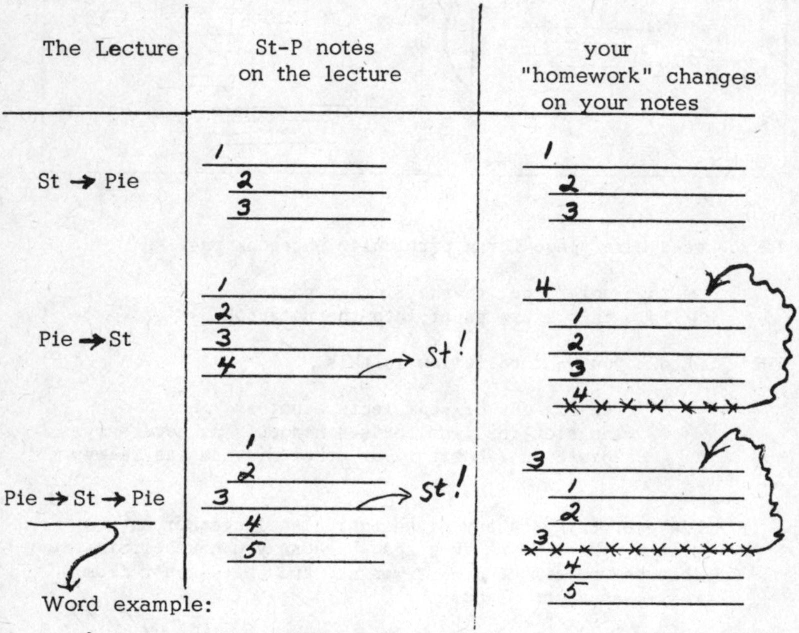

The Lecture	St-P notes on the lecture	your "homework" changes on your notes
St → Pie	1 2 3	1 2 3
Pie → St	1 2 3 4 → St!	4 1 2 3 4
Pie → St → Pie	1 2 3 4 5 → St!	3 1 2 3 4 5

Word example:

1 - John is very rational
2 - Robert is violent
3 - Story is the conflict between them
4 - John thinks change can come through reasoning
5 - Robert thinks the world changes only when forced

or, if you wish → 3 1 2 4 5

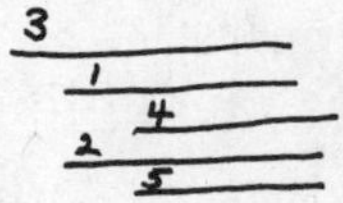

THING # 11

.. what to do when you have a professor who draws something on the board and talks about it at the same time?

.. This is important:

    .. write down the NAME of the something he is drawing.

    .. then write down what he SAYS ABOUT the something he is drawing.

    .. remember that the something he is drawing can be found in a book, or in the notes of a friend. But what this professor is saying about this something can't be found anywhere except in this lecture.

The professor says, "Now then, we come to the XQR cycle..." and starts drawing the structures and circles and arrows of the cycle

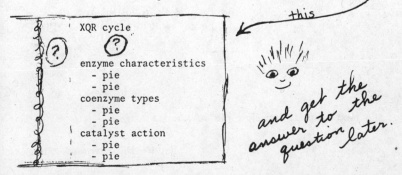

Meanwhile he is talking about such things as the enzyme characteristics, and the types of coenzymes (whatever they are) and the action of the catalyst...

If you are smart, you will write down this

XQR cycle
(?)
enzyme characteristics
- pie
- pie
coenzyme types
- pie
- pie
catalyst action
- pie
- pie

and get the answer to the question later.

THING # 12

.. what about diagrams that the Instructor hands out?

ANSWER

.. sort of the same as THING # 11 -- label the names
and parts of the diagram on the handout sheet,

> BUT
> ↳ write down what the instructor says about the
> diagram in your notes.

> - you see, if you try to jam it all onto
> the diagram sheet, you will leave out
> a great deal that the instructor says
> BECAUSE when you don't have space to
> write something down, your mind
> blocks out hearing it.

We are not discussing what Professors
and genius-type students
do in lectures. . .
they do not have THINGS.

they have instincts and intuitions.

they LIKE to study.

and they make a THING out of
people who don't like to study.
... like me

.. the next page is an example of how to

handle the diagram-Thing.

DIAGRAM -- in Handout given in lecture

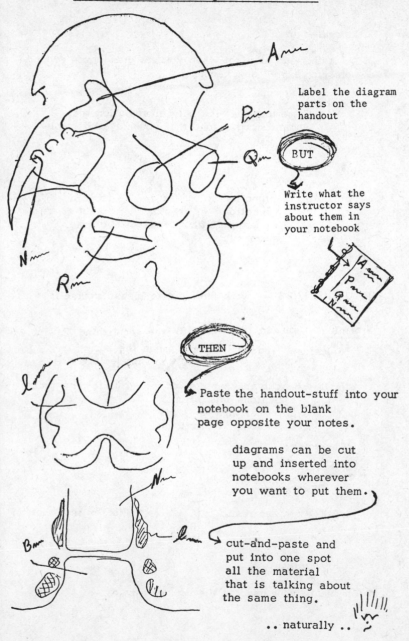

Label the diagram
parts on the
handout

BUT

Write what the
instructor says
about them in
your notebook

THEN

Paste the handout-stuff into your
notebook on the blank
page opposite your notes.

diagrams can be cut
up and inserted into
notebooks wherever
you want to put them.

cut-and-paste and
put into one spot
all the material
that is talking about
the same thing.

.. naturally ..

THING # 13

.. Abbreviations ? ? ?

.. Make them up <u>at night</u> when you are going over your
   notes for a St-P check-out.

> .. remember that the only abbreviation that
>   is any good is one that you are comfortable
>   with.

> .. for example   *yours*   *mine*

- function	fnc	func
- reaction	rxn	react
- characteristic	char	charac
- example	eg	i.e.

.. ODDS AND ENDS -- work them out to please yourself

<u>Example</u>: - you get two words for the same thing

"delusions" and "distortions" mean the same
to this lecturer...

✔ write one out and put the other near it in parenthesis
   - delusions (distortions)
✔ or use an equal sign
   - delusions = distortions

<u>Example</u>:

- Listing things ...

✔ Riots are result of	A	✔ Riots = result of	
	B		A
	C		B
			C

. whatever is
comfortable to your mind is the correct way to

St-Pie it.

THING # 14

.. rhetorical questions ? ? ?

    - (that's when the instructor puts a statement
     in the form of a question. He doesn't expect
     anyone to answer it...)

    - example:
      - " Now, then, what is it exactly that a
        cell does ?"

turn all rhetorical questions into
Statements as best you can. But do
it at night during your St-P checkout...
if you try it during lecture you will
lose the lecture content
         and it will serve you right...

Example

Rhetorical question: " Now then, what is it exactly that
               a cell does ?"

Turned into a St

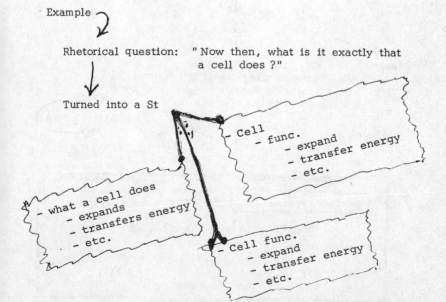

- Cell
  - func.
    - expand
    - transfer energy
  - etc.

- what a cell does
  - expands
  - transfers energy
  - etc.

- Cell func.
  - expand
  - transfer energy
  - etc.

A NON-THING PAGE

It is best to read these
THINGS-Units once a week
until you can

- read each Thing, (but not the answer)

- scribble down what you think
                the answer is

- and check your answers with mine.

Try it now with THING # 8, the Slot-ins . . .

"feeling" like you know a thing
    isn't the same as checking it out to see
        if you actually do know it, or if you are out
            on the usual S-H-T

                        Student - Hallucinating - Trip

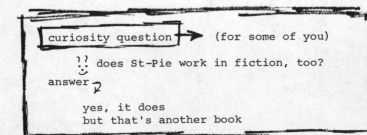

curiosity question ➤ (for some of you)

    ⁇ does St-Pie work in fiction, too?

answer

        yes, it does
        but that's another book

THING # 15

  .. How do I keep my notes looking neat if I am
    zilching and squnching things up ?

Answer

      Do not waste your time on such nonsense.

      Neatness is completely unimportant.

      No one sees your notes but you and God and
           God is too busy to bother with such trivia.

      You are no longer in grade school.

      Get down what the instructor says and get it
           down correctly.

      It is no comfort to be called "The neatest C minus
           in the class."

The only thing of importance to anyone is your performance.
You get no points for 'effort' now.

               This is the outside world..

    ... and no one cares how long
               or   you study
          how hard

(only you)

        (and me)

Goodbye — you better take a rest for a while period now.

" REST PAGE "

We are now going to St-Pie a lecture.

Get some paper and a pencil.
I have typed out the Instructor's lecture.
You are to use RECORDING ST-PIE on these notes
- Zilch & Margin freely
- use symbols, abbreviations
- forget about spelling

(spelling is for later).

IT DOES NOT MATTER IF YOU DO NOT
UNDERSTAND THE WORDS IN THE LECTURE.

IT DOES NOT MATTER IF YOU DO NOT
UNDERSTAND THE MEANING OF THE LECTURE.

I don't understand it either.
But you can still St-Pie it.

And after you have St-Pied it,
you usually understand it enough
to memorize it and pass the exam on it.

Don't forget,

After you have finished St-Pieing the lecture,

Do the Sentence Check-Out.

return to page 50 and
refresh your memory

or, if you prefer,
don't do the Sentence Check-Out
don't return to page 50
don't refresh your memory and
don't bother me...

... it's not MY problem

THE LECTURE

Very well, class, today we shall
be talking about body metabolism
and its measurement. You will
recall that earlier this year we
learned that the sum of all the
processes occurring in a cell or an
organism is called metabolism. The
constructive phase of metabolism
includes carbohydrate and protein
synthesis, while the destructive
phase includes oxidation and energy
release. The rate of metabolism
increases in proportion to the
increase in the activity of the
body. This activity may be muscular,
as in walking, running, or some
other form of exertion; or it
may be mental. Other factors
governing the metabolic rate include
exposure to cold and activity of
the digestive organs during
digestion of food. One way to
measure the metabolic rate of the
body is to measure the rate of
oxidation by determining the
amount of heat given off from the
body surface. This can be
measured by a device called a
calorimeter.

The person to be tested enters a
closed compartment that is equipped
to measure accurately all the heat given
off by his body. He may lie quietly
in bed during the process, or he may
sit in a chair and exercise vigour-
ously, depending on the nature of the
activity to be tested. The amount of
heat energy given off during each type
of activity is a direct indication
of the rate of oxidation in the
body tissues. Calorimeter tests are
important in determining the energy
needs of various individuals in order
to adjust a diet to their specific
requirements.

INSTRUCTIONS are to be
followed exactly, please.

① Write your Recording
St-Pie notes as if
you were "hearing" this
material in a lecture.

② Glance at my notes
of this lecture
(on the left side of
page 126).
It will interest
some of you to see how
different minds Zilch,
Margin, "hear" and
St-Pie differently.

③ Now do your HOMEWORK:
"go over" your notes
of the lecture, using the
Sentence Check-Out, and the
second trick on page 95.

Fix up your notes as
you would with a real set
of class notes.

④ Compare your
fixed-up notes
with my fixed-up notes
(on the right side of
page 126).

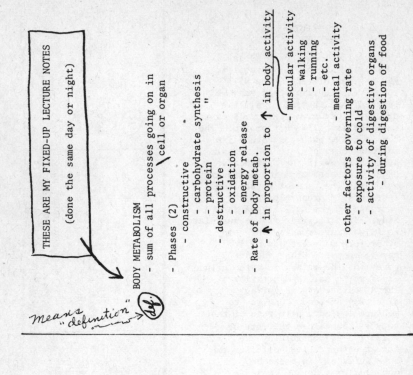

THESE ARE MY FIXED-UP LECTURE NOTES

(done the same day or night)

Means "definition" → def.

BODY METABOLISM
- sum of all processes going on in cell or organ
- Phases (2)
  - constructive
    - carbohydrate synthesis
    - protein "
  - destructive
    - oxidation
    - energy release
- Rate of body metab.
  - ↑ in proportion to ↑ in body activity
    - muscular activity
      - walking
      - running
      - etc.
    - mental activity
  - other factors governing rate
    - exposure to cold
    - activity of digestive organs
    - during digestion of food

THESE ARE MY LECTURE NOTES

Body Metab & measurment

Sum of all processes in [cell or organ] = metablism

- constructive phase
  [carbohydrate & protein] synthesis
- destructive phase
  - oxidation
  - energy release

Rate of metab
- ↑ in propor. to ↑ in body activity
  - may be muscular
    - walking
    - running
    - etc
  - may be mental
- other factors governing metab rate
  - exposure to cold

MEASUREMENT OF BODY METABOLISM
- Method: measure metabolic rate
  - by measuring rate of oxidation
  - determines amt. of heat given off from body surface
  - device = Calorimeter
- procedure
  - person to be tested enters closed compartment
    equipped to measure accurately all heat given off by body
  - person lies quiet in bed
    OR sits in chair
    OR exercises
    - depends on activity to be tested
  - amt. heat given off = direct indication of oxidation rate in body tissues
- Use of Calorimeter tests
  - determines energy needs of individs
  - can then adjust diet to needs of

(the factors)
activity of digestve organs
- during digest. of food

- measure metabolic rte
  - by mesure rate of oxidation
    - determines amt of heat given off by bdy surface
    - use device = calorimeter

person to be tested
- enters closed compartmnt
  equipped to mesure accurately all heat given off by bdy
- lies quiet in bed
  or sit in chair   in process
  or exercise
  - depends on activity to be tested
- amt of heat energy given off
  = direct indicatn of rate of oxid in bdy tissues

Calor. tests = important use
- determines energy needs of diff individs
- can then adjust diet to needs

Are you with me?

Good. We'll do one more thing with these notes.

    We know the notes are correct now,
and ready for exam studying.

    But there are so many lines of notes
that I can't get a general idea of the lecture,
the over-all organization of what was
talked about...this is what teachers want and

            ...are always calling "the big picture".

      Well, the "big picture" is just a
      St-Pie Summary of the first two or
      three indent levels of notes. That's all it is.

... We did this on
pages 72 & 73,

    but this lecture is
perfectly organized
and
      has no
      fuzz-areas.

For practice, you try to
St-Pie the first two or 3
indent levels of your
fixed-up notes.

    Or you can St-Pie the
first few levels of
my notes (on pages
126 & 127).

Now turn this page
upside-down and check
with my over-all
organization of the
lecture...which is a
St-Pie Summary of a
lecture (or of a
topic, or of a course)
using the Sentence
Check-Out, of course.

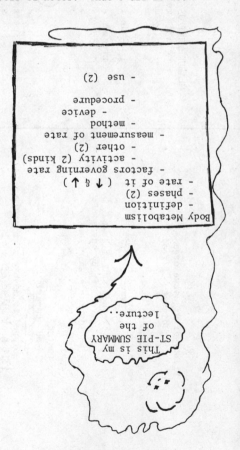

Okay, take a break.

Get a banana
or a peanut butter sandwich.

Lecture St-Pieing is a fancy
swan dive from the high board.

It might take a few
minutes to learn it.

SURVIVAL INFORMATION
for
LECTURE NOTE-TAKING

1. DO [NOT] CHANGE THE ORDER OF THE ST-PIE UNITS IN YOUR NOTES

    . keep the same sequence of information that you
    heard & recorded while the Instructor was talking.

2. DO [NOT] CHANGE THE LANGUAGE OF THE LECTURER

    . if he says gluggle, you say gluggle
    . if he says factors, you say factors (NOT causes).

When you are going over
your lecture notes, and
getting them into St-Pie form   This → "studying"

    . add in everything you can recall to fill out the notes
    . correct and fix-up your St-Pie indents as you see
    more clearly what the Instructor meant

    . BUT keep the order and the language of the lecture.

If you change the order
you are "reorganizing"
the lecture...

... and you don't
understand it well
enough to do that
yet.

If you change the language
you are "paraphrasing" what
the Instructor said...

If you do these things,
you are Selective St-Pieing,
which is fine for texts
but rotten for lectures.

AFTER you see clearly what the
Instructor's order or pattern
was,

and AFTER you understand what
he was talking about,

THEN you can put the stuff
into a pattern that suits your mind
if you want to:

You can re-copy the notes (yugh.)
Or you can cut & paste them (also yugh.)
Or you can just accept the pattern that is.

You don't have to
read the next page.
It is just me
blowing off steam.

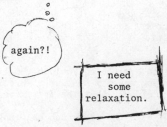

again?!

I need
some
relaxation.

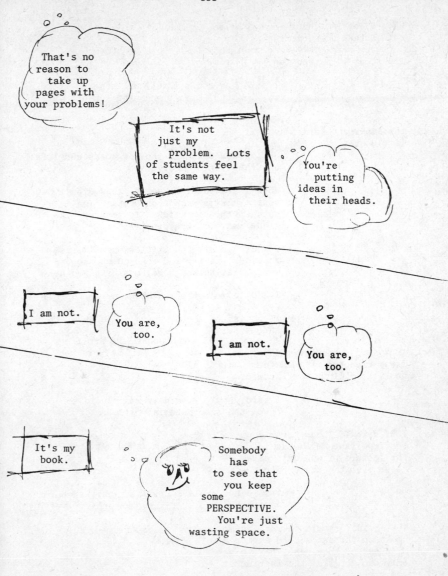

When I was in school THEY told me
not to take down everything the
lecturer said, only take down the
important ideas and the Key Words.

I said how could I tell what the Key Words
were, when I didn't know the subject yet?

Then THEY said the Key Words were
the important words, not all the
little ones.

So I wrote down all the big words and left
out the little ones.

When I read over my notes, they didn't make
sense. There wasn't any connection
between the big words. It sounded like
gibberish. It was gibberish.

I stuck in all the little words I could
remember, to try and connect up the big
words. It helped some, but not enough.

I had to read the textbook on the topic.

I complained about having to go over the
same material twice.

THEY said I was lazy, that
I was expected to read the
books to fill in the lecture.

I said, Why? I said it was stupid to
cover the same material twice.

THEY said if I had taken down
the Important Key Words in
the lecture, I wouldn't need
to go over the topic twice.

I said how could I tell what the Key Words
were, when I didn't know the subject yet?

THEY said I should be reading more
books on the subject to enrich my
mind and my knowledge, not to get
only the material the Instructor
was giving.

I gave up.
I quit listening to them and
started to take down
everything the lecturer said.

And that's what I suggest
to students.

Take down everything.
Take notes every minute of the lecture.

Besides daydreaming,
what else are you going to do with the time????

If you don't use the time to take notes,
you end up spending one hour
in class,

and another hour reading the same stuff
in a textbook, or filling in the outline
sheets the lecturer gave you,
or listening to the whole d--n thing
again on a tape recorder.

...which means you will have spent

two hours on one hour's
worth of material !??!

Phooey .

You can if you want to.
Not me.

SKIMMING A CHAPTER BEFORE A LECTURE, suggestion:

. Read the headings & italics aloud.
. Do this two or three times, but do it aloud.

(find someplace private so people
don't hear you mumbling to yourself..)

REASON:

When you skim headings silently
you get an eye-picture of the words.

For LECTURES you need to have a SOUND-SENSE
of the words.

Example: you <u>read</u> the heading:
MEIOSIS, OOPTOCEPHALIC PROBLEM

When the lecture is going on,
you <u>hear</u> these sounds

" MY OSIS IS IMPORTANT UP TO SEFALIK PROBLEMS "

While your mind is trying to fit the sounds to the
things you read,
   when you skimmed
   the headings silently,

        the lecturer is
giving a lot of facts about MY OSIS (meiosis) which are
not getting into your notes

     which means you'll have

     to read the text

     book,

       which makes you

       a time-waster..

What you need to do,
and what gets done by reading the Headings & Italics ALOUD

   is to learn the <u>sound</u> of the words the teacher
   is going to use.

   Even if you don't know how to spell the
   words, it doesn't matter. When you
   hear them in lecture, you are
   familiar with them

     You know you can go to the text and find
     them later, to spell out properly.

So, during the lecture, you can scribble
anything that will recall the word to
you later.

   Then, during your nightly fix-ups
   find the word in the text, and paste it into your
           notes.

THIS WHOLE PROCEDURE TAKES ONLY

ABOUT TEN MINUTES TIME

BEFORE A LECTURE...

> and besides making your Mind able to hear
> what the teacher is saying,
>
> there's a funny, added spin-off.

For some reason I don't understand, when you read the text
this way <u>three</u> times, you not only know the words that are
going to come at you,

> but you also have a "sense" of the
> whole topic.
>
> It is most peculiar.
> Try it a couple of times and see.

Note: the first few times you do this
read-aloud bit, you feel like
an idiot, of course.

NOW LET'S LOOK AT

The   School-Language Business

How to use St-Pie to understand what <u>THEY</u> want.

THE PROBLEM OF "ABSTRACT-THINKING"

. Try using my system?

School people talk about different "levels of organization"

- they say a student should be able to go from
  the "factual level" of organizing & understanding material
     to
  the "abstract level" of organizing & understanding material.

- they say a student should learn how to do abstract-thinking.

  I never did understand what they meant by
  "abstract thinking". Sometimes I think lots of people
  who use those words, also don't understand what it means.

              . HOWEVER, I have solved the problem
                though I am still not sure what the
                words mean:

        I do everything backwards:
        First I use the St-Pie techniques,
        then I translate the St-Pie stuff
        back into their language, if they ask for it.

. If they ask for the "factual level" of stuff,

        I give them the St-Pie Units.

. If they ask for the "classification level"

        . "please classify this material"
        . "put this content into the proper categories"
        . "underline the Key Words"

        I give them the Go-Betweens

              which we are going to do in the
                                next section.

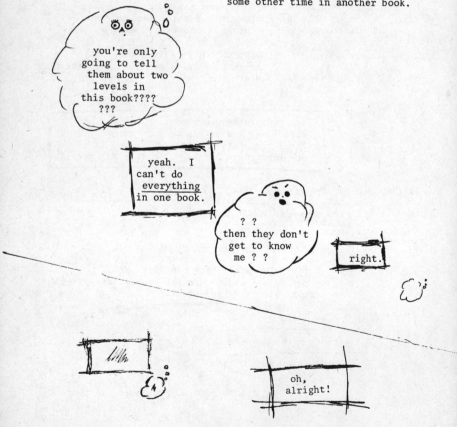

If they ask for

     - the Important Ideas
     - the Concepts
     - the Generalizations
     - a Precis, or a Summary of the content
     - or an Abstract

I give them the Over-All-Organization

which is the OAO

which we are not going to do in
this book, but which we will do
some other time in another book.

you're only
going to tell
them about two
levels in
this book????
???

yeah. I
can't do
everything
in one book.

? ?
then they don't
get to know
me ? ?

right.

oh,
alright!

You can make a pretty good OAO
this way

(1) Make a St-Pie Summary of your notes (see pages 72 & 128).

(2) Do a Sentence Check-Out on it.

(3) Correct it until it all checks out okay.

(4) Read it off in sentences, or write it...

and sound frightfully smart, like this (for page 128)

> The lecture was on Body Metabolism. The term was
defined. The two phases of the process were described.
The increase and decrease of body metabolism rate is
governed by four factors.

> The measurement of the rate of body metabolism is
done by a specific method and procedure, the Calorimeter
tests. Measurement of the rate has two uses: determining
the energy needs of an ididividual, and adjusting diets
of individuals.

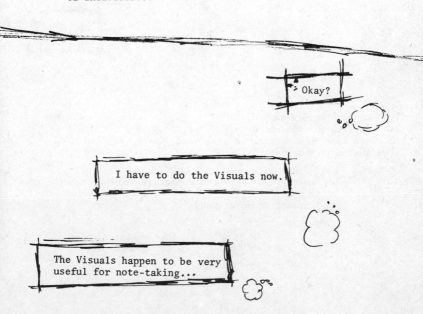

Okay?

I have to do the Visuals now.

The Visuals happen to be very
useful for note-taking...

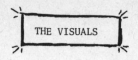

THE VISUALS

(Frankly, I hate writing
 this part of the book.)

you hate
writing
practically
all of
it.

you shouldn't
say things like that.

why
shouldn't I?
I'm not going
to get a chance
to talk later

GET OFF
THE PAGE

VISUALS is a word I made up.
It refers to the kind of material
that you have to visualize in your head,
like anatomy, or geometry,

> where you need to see a picture of it
> in your mind,
> in order to understand it.

> Some people can make a mental "picture" as
> they read the words of a Visual.

> Some people can't. I can't.

I can remember ideas and
pieces of ideas, fairly easily,

but there isn't a prayer in heaven or hell
that can make my mind understand or
remember material like this
if I just <u>read</u> it.

> "Oxygen is absorbed by the lung capillaries,
> where it combines with the hemoglobin of
> the red blood corpuscles. In the tissues,
> where the concentration of Oxygen is low,
> hemoglobin releases its oxygen."

> I can read it six times and
> gradually the ONLY THING that
> happens is that I BECOME a
> "corpuscle hemoglobin concen-
> trate of Oxygen releasing."

If I have to study Visual stuff,

> I have to make
> my own personal sketch of the words
>
> as I read them.

It does not do me any good to read
the words and follow the TEXTBOOK
pictures.

THEIR pictures are very beautiful,
and very clear, but they
will not stay in my head.

> For me, everybody else's picture
> is a Transplant. After twenty
> minutes, my mind throws it out.

It is only MY rotten drawings that I
wouldn't show to a dawg,
that make an image form in my
head, and stay there.

TEXT MATERIAL   ...which, if I try just reading, is hopeless.

The organs of external respiration.
     The first group of these organs
includes the passages through which air
travels in reaching the bloodstream:
the nostrils, nasal passages, pharynx,
trachea, bronchi, bronchial tubes and
lungs.
     Air enters the nose in two streams,
because the nostrils are separated by
the septum. From the nostrils, air
enters the nasal passages which lie
above the mouth cavity. The nostrils
contain hairs that aid in filtering
dirt out of the air. Other foreign
particles may lodge on the moist mucous
membranes in the nasal passages. The
length of the nasal passages warms the
air and adds moisture to it before it
enters the trachea. All these advantages
of nasal breathing are lost in mouth
breathing.
     From the nasal cavity, the air
passes through the pharynx and enters
the windpipe or trachea. The upper end
of the trachea is protected by a carti-
laginous flap, the epiglottis. During
swallowing, the end of the trachea is
closed by the epiglottis. At other
times, the trachea remains open to
permit breathing. The larynx, or Adam's
apple, is the enlarged upper end of the
trachea. Inside it are the vocal cords.
The walls of the trachea are supported
by horseshoe-shaped rings of cartilage
that hold it open for the free passage
of air. The trachea and its branches
are lined with cilia. These are in
constant motion and carry dust or dirt
taken in with air upward toward the
mouth. This dust, mixed with mucus, is
removed when you cough, sneeze, or clear
your throat.
     From the trachea the air moves
into the right bronchus and the left
bronchus.

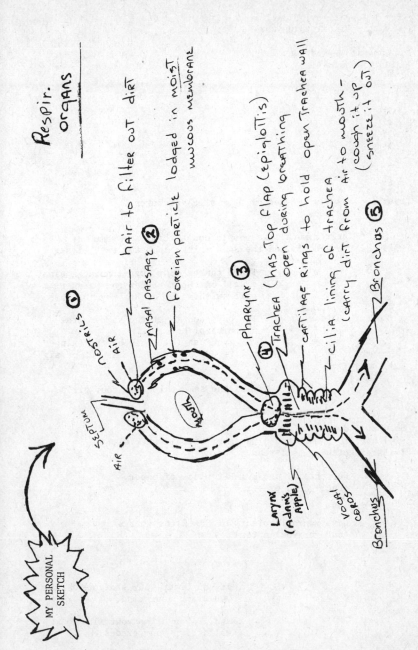

MY PERSONAL SKETCH

Respir. organs

① nostrils

hair to filter out dirt

nasal passage ②

Foreign particle lodged in moist mucous membrane

SEPTUM

AIR

AIR

MOUTH

Pharynx ③

Trachea (has top flap (epiglottis) open during breathing ④

cartilage rings to hold open trachea wall

cilia lining of trachea (carry dirt from air to mouth — cough it up / sneeze it out)

Bronchus ⑤

Larynx (Adam's apple)

vocal cords

Bronchus

For a long time I didn't know
why this Visual thing worked.

I knew it worked, but I
didn't know why.

      Then I finally figured it out.

I think
that
everyone has his own mental (symbolic) pictures
of things he sees,

      pretty much like people don't think the same way
      they don't see the same things the same way, either.

          . There can be four boys leaning against
            a wall in the corridor and watching a
            girl swishing by on her way to class.

          . The boys don't get the same mental
            pictures of her.
              - you can tell this by the things
                they say after she is out of sight.

          ...and the same thing for four girls.

So what I do,
if I have to understand & remember Visual material,
I start sketching as I read.

      For this, I use a LARGE piece of paper,
      pencil, and eraser.

      Give yourself plenty of SPACE for your sketches
      (and for your notes).

          . remember,

          . if you cramp your sketches & notes
            you cramp your mind,

          . and if you cramp your mind, you
            will crimp your grades.

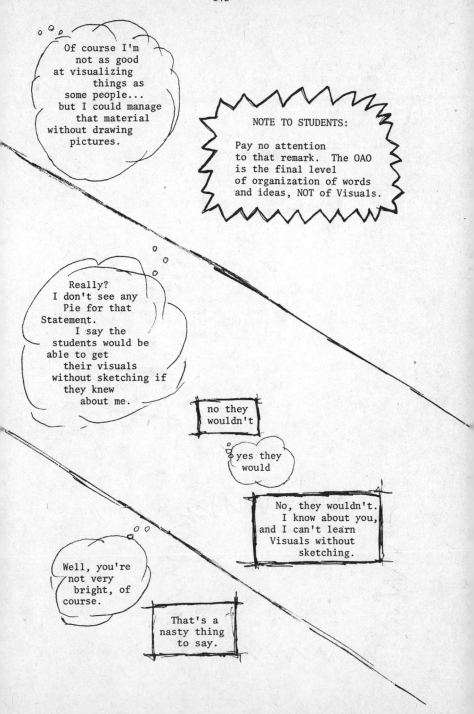

146

TEXTBOOK MATERIAL

Each living cell takes in oxygen, uses it in the oxidation
of foods, and gives off carbon dioxide and water. This
vital process supplies the cell with energy to carry on
its life processes.

SPACE for your PERSONAL SKETCH #1

. make your sketch as you read,

. then check your sketch with
  mine on page 150.

148

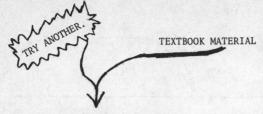

TEXTBOOK MATERIAL

The nose and nasal passages:

Air enters the nose
in two streams, because
the nostrils are separated
by the septum. From the
nostrils, air enters the
nasal passages which lie
above the mouth cavity.
The nostrils contain
hairs that aid in fil-
tering dirt out of the
air. Other foreign par-
ticles may lodge on the
moist mucous membranes in
the nasal passages. The
length of the nasal pass-
ages warms the air and
adds moisture to it be-
fore it enters the trachea.
All these advantages
of nasal-breathing are
lost in mouth-breathing.

The trachea:

From the nasal cavity,
the air passes through the
pharynx and enters the
windpipe, or trachea. The
upper end of the trachea
is protected by a cartilagi-
nous flap, the epiglottis.

During swallowing, the end
of the trachea is closed by
the epiglottis.

SPACE for your PERSONAL SKETCH #2

. Sketch as you read.

. Erase, erase, erase as you go.

. When finished, check with my
  sketch on page 151.

The trick about this Visuals thing
is that you have to experiment.

You just have to fool around and see
what sort of things are Visuals to you.

For some people, VISUALS ARE

. anything with a "structure", like bones, or governments

. or things that are a "process", like what goes on in a
or what goes on during a social change.   \cell,

For some people, VISUALS ARE

. to compare  things, like types of animals with
their special characteristics,

. or anything to do with the 'mechanism' of how something
works, like how a bunch of different stresses bring about
a psychological change in a person.

You have to find your own Visuals,
BUT DO NOT SHOW YOUR SKETCHES
to other people...

- sketches are only to make the material clear to you,
- and give you a personalized brain imprint, ready for
\exam-time review.

Sketching is nice because it lets
you tell your Unconscious Mind to
go eat worms. You are learning
consciously, which makes you the
boss of your own School-Thinking.

Remember, only you and
God are going to see
your sketches, and God
doesn't care how you
learn your school work.

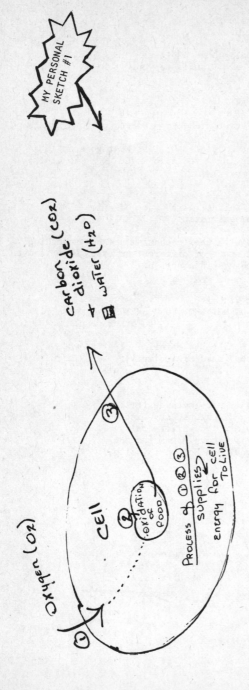

MY PERSONAL SKETCH #1

The sketch is correct, but as it stands it has a PROBLEM. It needs a TITLE. It is a serious error to make sketches without giving them titles.

Think about it. In another month or two, when you need to prepare for or review for an exam... how will you know what the purpose of the sketch

was supposed to be? The structures of a cell? Gas exchange in a cell?

Re-read the material on page 147 and pick yourself a title for your sketch

.. The process a Cell goes through?
.. Activity in a cell?
.. Energy source for a cell?

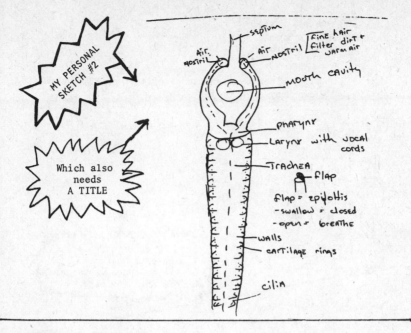

MY PERSONAL SKETCH #2

Which also needs A TITLE

TO PREPARE FOR EXAMS

(1) Cover the sketch with a sheet of paper and look only at the title of this Visual.

(2) Reproduce the sketch from memory. Sketch very, very, very quickly.

> During exams you will be making these "fast sketches" for information recall.

(3) Check your fast-sketch with the original Visual.

(4) In red crayon, CORRECT your fast-sketch. Include all omissions or errors.

> You now know what your mind has already memorized, and what you still need to memorize.

(5) Repeat steps 1 through 4 until you have the fast-sketch about 90% correct.

> Do not, repeat not, try for 100%.

> Thank you.

Visuals and St-Pie Units
are the first steps in
learning how to study.

   - If you don't intend to experiment to find your
     own hangups with the Visuals,

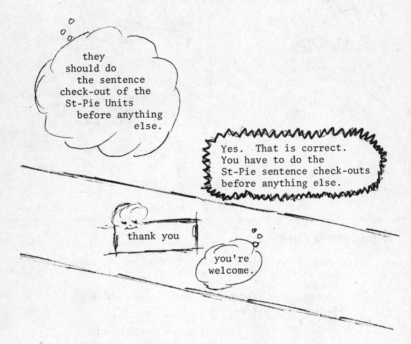

they
should do
   the sentence
check-out of the
St-Pie Units
   before anything
             else.

Yes. That is correct.
You have to do the
St-Pie sentence check-outs
before anything else.

thank you

you're
welcome.

   - and if you aren't going to keep the order and
     the language of the Lectures in your St-Pie
     fix-ups...

Then you are trying to
make like a genius,

and if you aren't one, all you'll
get out of your paraphrasing
and reorganizing
is a mess of exam trouble,

              which you will deserve. Because you
              have no right to paraphrase and
              reorganize someone until you <u>know</u>
              what he said.

You have to practice.

The mind is a muscle
like everything else.

      If you get a charley-horse
      of the brain when you are
      exercising it,
               do not worry. It will
               go away.

        Take a hot bath, and say to yourself
        over & over,

           "While I am practicing how to
           study, I am learning the
           material for my next exam."

      (This does **not** always help, but you can try it.)

If you DON'T intend to practice, then

        ... go use someone else's note-taking system

           St-Pie won't work for you.

      The rest of you can come with me to the Go-Betweens
      which some people
      call the Gee-Bees (G-B's).

THE

GO-BETWEENS

ARE

THE

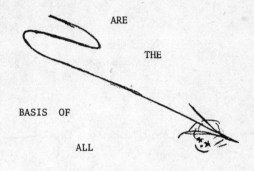

BASIS OF

ALL

ORGANIZATION

ORGANIZATION

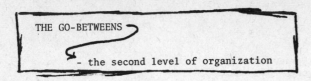

THE GO-BETWEENS

- the second level of organization

By now you St-Pied for an hour
every day (in order to make life
easier for yourself)...

you practiced Selective St-Pie
         & Recording (lecture) St-Pie

you found your own Visuals
        and made your own sketches for them

. you checked out your Statements & Pie
      by making sure they made sense-sentences

If you didn't...
      ...that is okay,

but it means you aren't taking St-Pie proper notes,

and you will only be wasting your time trying
to work on this section.

I am sorry about this, but

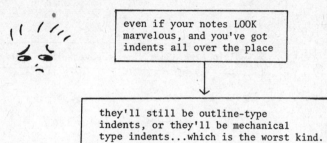

even if your notes LOOK
marvelous, and you've got
indents all over the place

they'll still be outline-type
indents, or they'll be mechanical
type indents...which is the worst kind.

Nothing is worse than mechanical-type
indents. It is better to leave your
notes without indents altogether.

If your notes aren't
St-Pied, you can get into a
mess of trouble with the G-B's

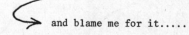

and blame me for it.....

... so some other system will
really be much better for you,
and you ought to try one of them.

Thank you.

However, if you CAN St-Pie textbooks & lecture notes correctly,

you have reached the next hurdle on the road to academic survival

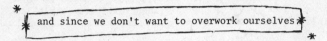

and since we don't want to overwork ourselves

the best way to get over
the hurdle is
to let the Instructor
carry us over.

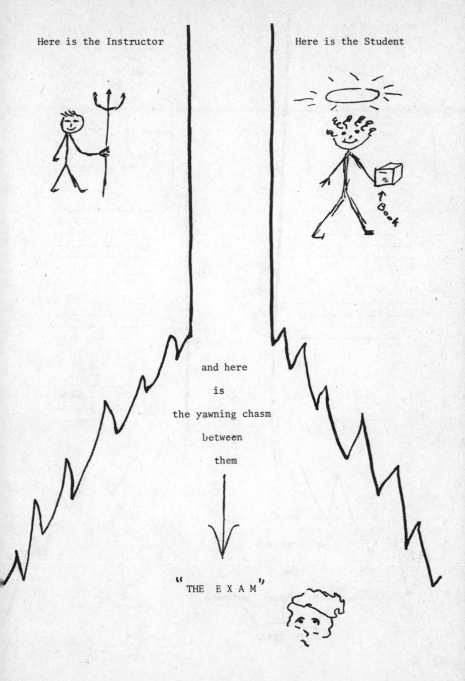

You already know
that the Professor
talks in St-Pie

even though he
doesn't know
what he's doing

THE INSTRUCTOR

And you take notes
in St-Pie

so what HE said,
you got down during
the lecture

THE STUDENT

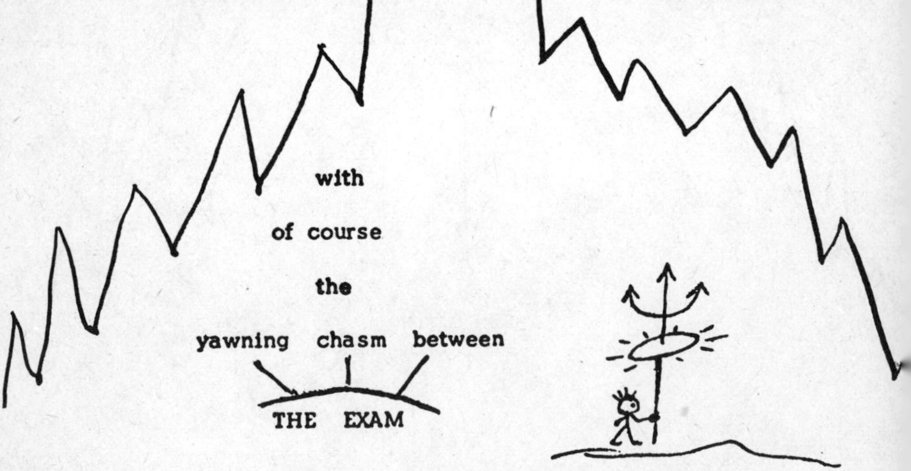

with

of course

the

yawning chasm between

THE EXAM

The Instructor has lectured.
The Student has taken notes.

The Instructor is now at Making-up-the-Exam time. He wants to
know if the Student knows this tidbit.

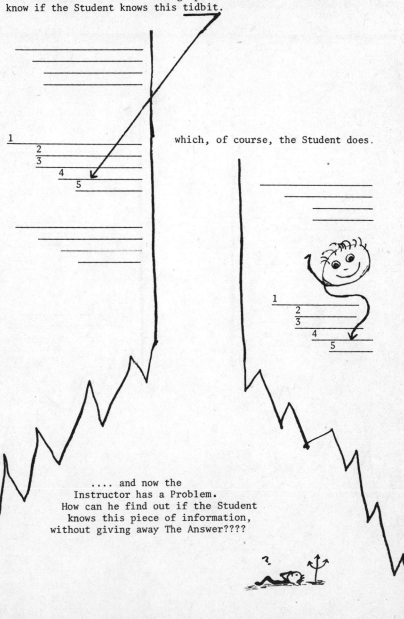

which, of course, the Student does.

.... and now the
Instructor has a Problem.
How can he find out if the Student
knows this piece of information,
without giving away The Answer????

When an Instructor has a Problem, his Unconscious Mind begins
to talk to his Conscious Mind like this: "Now, let me see.
This stuff is actually talking about the mechanism of the
digestive process.   So....."

So he

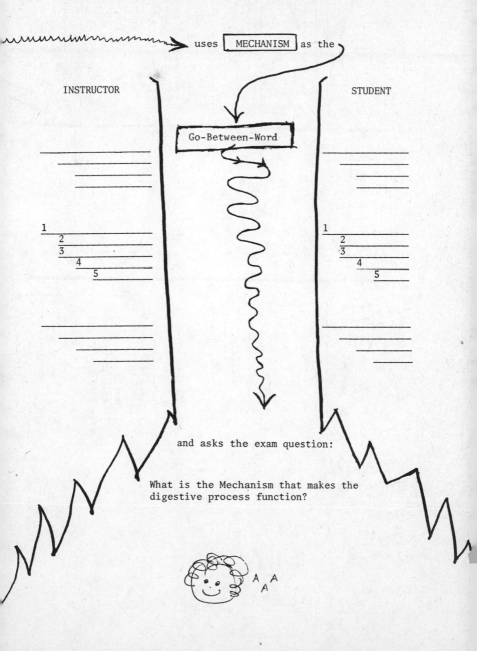

uses MECHANISM as the

INSTRUCTOR

STUDENT

Go-Between-Word

1
2
3
4
5

1
2
3
4
5

and asks the exam question:

What is the Mechanism that makes the
digestive process function?

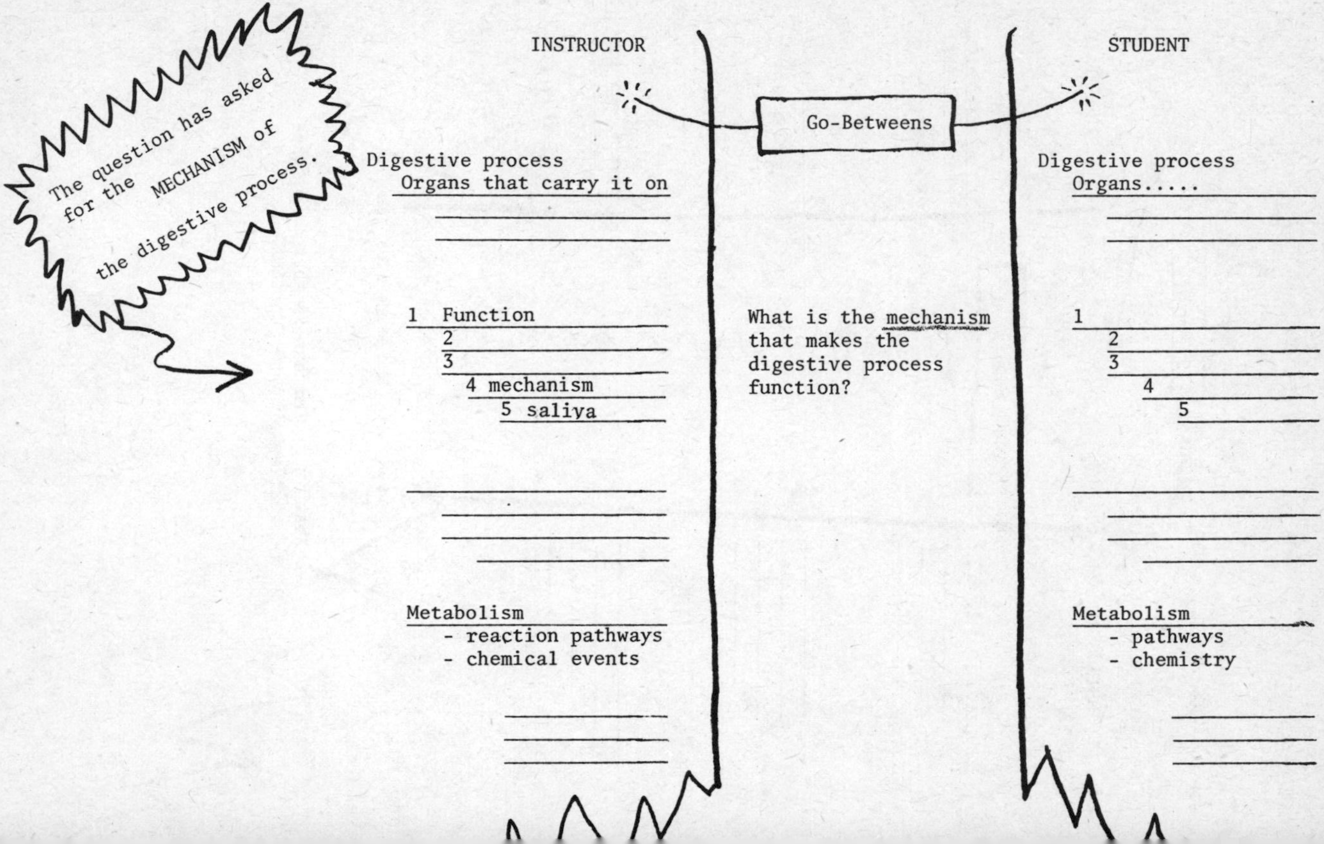

166

STUDENT

Go-Betweens

INSTRUCTOR

What is the mechanism
that makes the
digestive process
function?

Digestive process
Organs......

1
2
3
4
5

Metabolism
- pathways
- chemistry

Digestive process
Organs that carry it on

1 Function
2
3
4 mechanism
5 saliva

Metabolism
- reaction pathways
- chemical events

The question has asked
for the MECHANISM of
the digestive process.

167

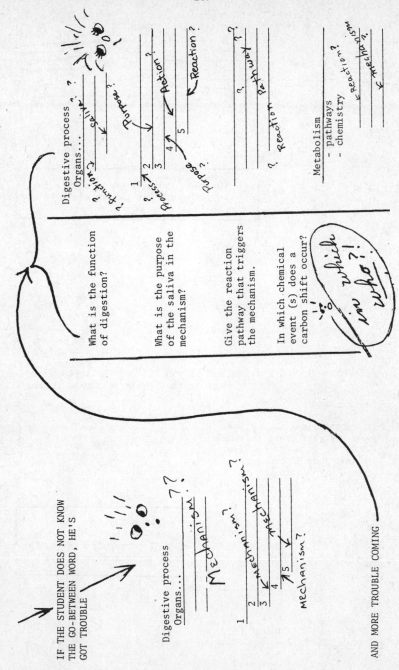

IF THE STUDENT DOES NOT KNOW
THE GO-BETWEEN WORD, HE'S
GOT TROUBLE

What is the function
of digestion?

What is the purpose
of the saliva in the
mechanism?

Give the reaction
pathway that triggers
the mechanism.

In which chemical
event(s) does a
carbon shift occur?

AND MORE TROUBLE COMING

There must be an easier way to live....I think???

There is

> But ∿→ you have to recognize that everyone has his own special G-B's.

.. some people think of the Go-Betweens

             as
       "classifications"
            or
        "categories"
            or
      "subject-matter"

                  .. and if you like any of those words
                     better than G-B's, use them instead.

.. only remember that whatever
   name you give them, they all
   act as Go-Betweens between
   you and your Instructors

> SO ∿→ you must get into
> your St-Pie notes the G-B's
> of THAT particular Instructor
> in THAT particular course...

The Go-Betweens are a little different

  from Categories & Classifications & Subject-Matter

because the G-B's can be ... a word
.   . a phrase
.   or
.   . a sentence (whole one, or part)

CATEGORY CLASSIFICATION SUBJECT-MATTER	GO-BETWEENS
mechanism	(same)
mechanism of Protein Synthesis	(same)
-----------------	Mechanism by which the synthesis of proteins is carried out in the XYZ cycle

large-size word for subject or course.

zilch

Every discipline...History, Biology Journalism, Chemistry, etc....has its own G-B's and its own special definitions for the G-B it uses

Every instructor in any given discipline has his own special way of using the Go-Between or classification-words in his own special course.

Example:
"Composition" in a Biology course does not mean the same meaning as "Composition" in an English course.

#1 is talking about the pieces that make up the whole thing (blood, kidneys, veins, etc.)

#2 is the whole thing you are supposed to make up from the pieces (the Statements & Pies of a theme)

Using your own G-B's is called 'freedom of thought'
or
'freedom of speech'

which is a Good Thing...

... except when it messes you up???
... or when you mess up someone else with it???

Now, one way to stay out of the Exam Mess situation,
is to understand what an Instructor's exam question
is asking for.

It is one of the REQUIREMENTS for understanding an exam question

this is a
G-B word

that
you know the G-B's of
THAT Instructor in
THAT particular course.

To learn the G-B's in any course,

your ears and your mind must
be trained to recognize them;

Just as you trained your ears
and your mind to recognize
the St-Pie Units,

.. and your fingers must add
the G-B's into your lecture notes,
using the same practice
system as with the St-Pieing
of your texts & lectures.

Suppose you don't do this ?

you could spend an awful lot of time
reading, and an awful lot of time
memorizing, and still come out with
an exam grade that wasn't worth all
that time and work . . . . .

BECAUSE

If the Instructor called column A "CHEMICAL REACTION"

and you thought of it as CHEMICAL ACTION

	column A	column B	column C
His G-B's	Chemical reaction		
Your G-B's	Chemical action		

and the Instructor said columns B & C were

talking about | CHEMICAL ACTION
&
PRODUCT

but you wrote down that columns B & C were

PRODUCT & SYNTHESIS

... which you did because you were paraphrasing

(putting stuff in your own words)

... or because you were using G-B's you knew and liked from other courses and other Instructors.

	column A	column B	column C
His G-B's		Chemical action	Product
Your G-B's		Product	Synthesis

Then you may be on an
asphalt Freeway to Exam Troubles.

Because this is what happens

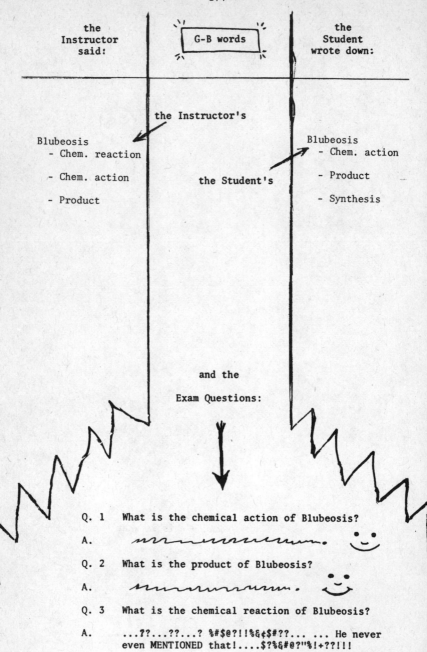

the Instructor said:

G-B words

the Student wrote down:

the Instructor's

Blubeosis
- Chem. reaction
- Chem. action
- Product

the Student's

Blubeosis
- Chem. action
- Product
- Synthesis

and the

Exam Questions:

Q. 1   What is the chemical action of Blubeosis?

A.

Q. 2   What is the product of Blubeosis?

A.

Q. 3   What is the chemical reaction of Blubeosis?

A.   ...??...??...? %#$@?!!%&¢$#??... ... He never
even MENTIONED that!....$?%&#@?"%!+??!!!

and the RESULT ➘

EXAM credit received by the student:

Q. 1   zero
Q. 2   zero
Q. 3   zero

"...and after all that studying, too!
Dammit, the more I study, the worse grades I get."

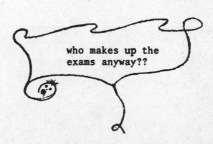

So next time don't "study" so
much, and spend 20 minutes on
each lecture adding the
Instructor's Go-Betweens into
your St-Pie notes.

who makes up the
exams anyway??

Sometimes you should
think about the Instructor's Problem

If he's got a class of
twenty or a hundred students

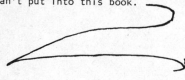

he's got twelve or forty different types
of minds with different types of Go-Betweens
to lecture at

and no matter whose G-B's
he uses, the rest of the class
are going to call him a rotten
lecturer or a rotten teacher or
DISORGANIZED, or other names
I can't put into this book.

So he might as well
use his own G-B's....

... which he does, anyway,
even though he doesn't
know that's what he's
doing.

But since life is easier if
you know what you're doing

THIS IS THE TECHNIQUE FOR FINDING G-B's AND
ADDING THEM INTO YOUR NOTES

> You point to any item of your St-Pie notes and you
> say, "This stuff is talking about . . . . "
>
> The dot, dot, dots is the Go-Between word.

YOU CAN HAVE GO-BETWEENS for an item
                                                      &
                                            for a St-Pie Unit
                                                      &
                                            and for a bunch of St-Pie Units
                                                      &
                                            and for Conversation-with-People

The Go-Between for the item, or the Unit, etc.
then becomes the Statement for the item, Unit, or etc.

Go-Between
- item
	Go-Between
	- Statement
	     - Pie
	     - Pie

.... and that's how it should be written into your notes.

Some people have the mistaken idea
that you need to understand something
before you can G-B it.

        But actually, it's a back & forth
        thing... the G-B's help you check out
        the St-Pies, and the St-Pies help you
        think out the G-B's

                    keep it loose in your
                    head while you're
                    fooling around with
                    the G-B's & your notes.

Here are good St-Pie notes,
taken during a lecture on
something called "Lamina propria".

The student is about to do
his one-hour of homework.

He will do the St-Pie check-out
and the G-B's.

He is not happy about it, but
he is going to do it anyway.

→ 'item #1

Lamina propria   1
 - filled with small blood vessels   2
 - connects other layers   3
 - transportation of nutrients   4
 - defense   5
   - lumen is part of outside world   6
   - contains lymph nodules   7

The student points
to item #1 and begins
to mumble.....

.. item #1 is talking about-- that's what it's talking about "lamina propria"....that's the lecture topic.

Correct. There is no G-B for this item

.. item #2 is talking about what lamina propria is filled with... what Lamina propria is made up of...

item #2 is talking about the COMPOSITION of lamina propria.

Correct. Write 'composition' as Statement for item #2, or scribble it lightly in the notebook margin.

When you are sure of the G-B's, write them firmly into your notes.

.. item #3 is talking about the location of lamina propria...or did he call this item one of the functions of lamina ??

I'll use LOCATION for now, and put a Question Mark in the margin, and ask someone.

This is a FUZZ AREA for you. One of the functions of the G-B's is to pin-point what you know, don't know, & what's fuzz.

This is the correct procedure for students in Fuzz Areas.

(next page, please)

Correct. Write it lightly into your notes as Statement for # 4 & 5.

.. items # 4 & 5 are talking about the FUNCTION of lamina propria.

Correct. Scribble lightly into notes as Statement for #6.

.. item #6 is talking about why lamina propria is a defense. Therefore, item #6 is talking about the REASON lamina propria is a defense.

Correct. Item #7 has been indented incorrectly. It belongs at the same level of indentation as item #6, because that is the way the Instructor was discussing/using the item "contains lymph nodules".

.. item #7 is talking about the composition of lamina propria again. But he gave it as one of the reasons that the lamina propria was a defense. So the G-B here is REASON.

Read all that again.

Fix the indent-level.

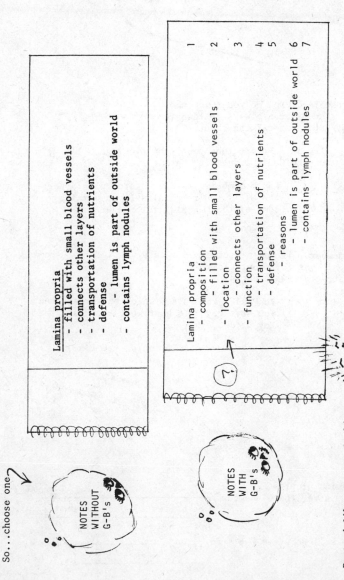

181

So...choose one

NOTES WITHOUT G-B's

Lamina propria
- filled with small blood vessels
- connects other layers
- transportation of nutrients
- defense
  - lumen is part of outside world
- contains lymph nodules

NOTES WITH G-B's

Lamina propria
- composition
  - filled with small blood vessels   1
- location   2
  - connects other layers   3
- function
  - transportation of nutrients   4
  - defense   5
    - reasons
      - lumen is part of outside world   6
      - contains lymph nodules   7

Pretend like you are looking at these notes just before your final exams.

Now you try writing the G-B's into
some notes of your own. Just keep
pointing to items and saying,
"This stuff is talking about..."

So's breathing. How do you think the
"smart" students can always tell what
the Instructor was talking about????

Try it. Before long you'll be picking
up the G-B's along with the St-Pies.

And remember...while you are going after
the G-B's you're painlessly memorizing
some of the material for the exam.

Also remember: if you practice G-B's half
an hour a night for about two weeks,
your Instructors will begin

to "talk" in G-B's...which only means that
you have begun to hear what they call the
Key Words.

Key Words = G-B's.

*It's a game;
it's only a game*

In 'Lamina propria'
we went after the G-B's for

each item in a St-Pie Unit

Now we will go after G-B's for

whole St-Pie Units

... after which you will be able to move around in your
notes, picking out G-B's for items or G-B's for
Units, as the situation demands:

... this is a nice way of saying: you will
learn how to grab an item here, a Unit there,
like you do with a jigsaw puzzle
and gradually, out of the cut-up mess,
you will put together
bits & pieces of ORGANIZED MATERIAL.

Then, the bits & pieces
begin to fit together,

and you're home free
with your mind grooving into the whole
School-Think bit...

Rest period.

TO FIND THE G-B's FOR WHOLE ST-PIE UNITS:

..pretend these are your notes
taken during a lecture

.pretend that they make no sense
at this moment; that they are just
a bunch of meaningless lines your
pencil scribbled while the
Instructor was talking about the Krebs Cycle.

GOING AFTER THE G-B's

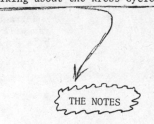

THE NOTES

Krebs Cycle

Section (1) is talking about the
FUNCTIONS of the Krebs cycle.
Three functions. Fncs = G-B

Section (2) is talking about the
STRUCTURES in the Krebs cycle.
Strs = G-B

Section (3) is talking about a
REACTION in the Krebs cycle.
Two reactions.
Rxn = G-B

Section (4) is talking about a
MECHANISM of the Krebs cycle...

...and so is section (5)..??

splat !

Nope. Wrong.

Sections 4 & 5 are not
talking about the mechanism of
the Krebs cycle..
..they are
talking about the MECHANISM OF
THE REACTIONS...(section 3) that
take place in the middle of the
Krebs cycle.

(1) Fncs
a ~~~
b ~~~
c ~~~

(2) Strs
str. a
str. b

str. c

(3) Rxn's
reaction x

reaction y

(4) Mech of
mechanism a

(5) Rxn's
mechanism b

.. so they're the mechanism of section 3 ??
......Okay, that's not so bad..

steam from
over-heating
of brain.

.. now I add the G-B's to
the notes....it's a good
thing I left that space
between the St-Pie Units...

Zilch & abbreviate just enough so it is clear to you.

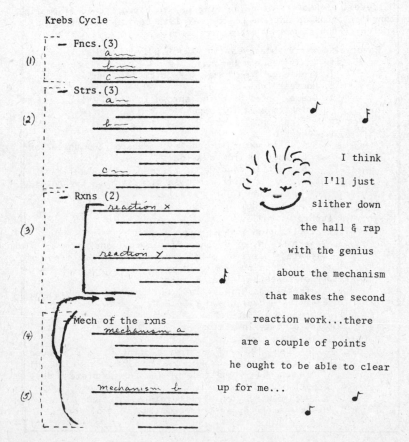

Krebs Cycle

(1) Fncs.(3)
  a
  b
  c

(2) Strs.(3)
  a
  b
  c

(3) Rxns (2)
  reaction x
  reaction y

(4) Mech of the rxns
  mechanism a

(5) mechanism b

I think

I'll just

slither down

the hall & rap

with the genius

about the mechanism

that makes the second

reaction work...there

are a couple of points

he ought to be able to clear

up for me...

HOW TO COMBINE USING

G-B's of ITEMS
&
G-B's of UNITS

. This is a set of notes taken during lecture by a student.
. The student got good grades, but spent a lot of time studying

"Ancient World 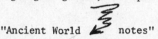 notes"

Sept. 29 Professor Shotwell

Only former authority for knowledge of ancient world - Herodotus and Bible
    Scientific Method
        1. Ancient stone -- key
Discovery of Rosetta stone, giving key to hieroglyphic & demotic language opens up antique history -- 19th century, knowledge of antiquity <u>now</u> gained by actual research

  Egypt discovered solar year in 4241 B.C., July 19
    1. Life in Thebes and Memphis
      1. Knowledge from remains -- pictures, etc.
      2. Houses high
      3. Grain sorted by being thrown in air
      4. Trinkets used for money
    Age of Unification.
      1. Causes of:
        A. Nile-natural road-way, means of communication
        B. Shut in from outsiders
        C. Fertile country
            (Diff. in case of Assyria. Euphrates
            open to ingress.)

History of Euphrates Valley
    I. First civilization in Egypt for reasons:
      1. Desert, means of defense from barbarians
      2. Climate - easy for primative people without means of
          protection from cold -
   II. History of Lower Valley of Euphrates.
      1. As fertile as Nile Valley, but open to attack.
      2. Elamites - overthrown 2000 B.C.
      3. Supremacy of Babylon -
      Commercial city in plains
          a. Khammurabi
            (Dec. 1901 - French excavating in Persia found
            stone set up by Kham. with picture of King and
            sun god -- and code of laws -- complete oldest
      4. Assyrians
         a. Recorded Babylonian literature
      5. Medes - broke up Assyrian empire; control north.

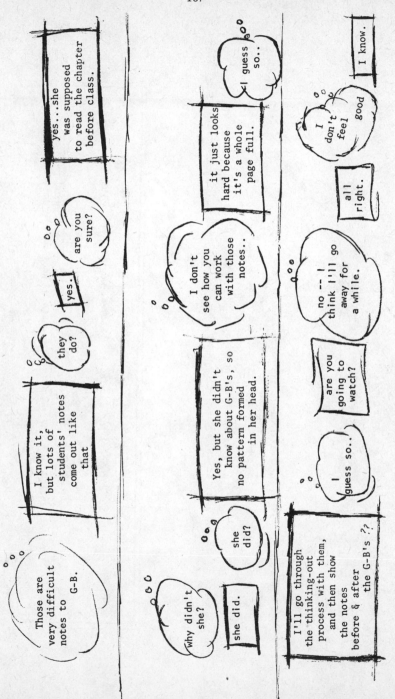

the G-B's

On these next pages are the "Ancient World notes" again.

The numbers at each line are for reference, so you can follow my thinking-out process in finding the G-B's.

I will do this process on pages 190 & 191.
You follow what I do.

On pages 192 & 193 are the notes BEFORE and AFTER finding the G-B's.

Some of you might want to look first at pages 192 & 193, to convince yourself it is worthwhile following the thinking process.

Then come back here.
I'll wait.

Sept. 29 Professor Shotwell

1   Only former authority for knowledge of ancient world -- Herodotus
2   and Bible
3   Scientific Method
4   1. Ancient stone -- key
5   Discovery of Rosetta stone, giving key to hieroglyphic and demotic language
6   opens up antique history -- nineteenth century, knowledge of antiquity now
7   gained by actual research

8 Egypt discovered solar year in 4241 B.C., July 19
9   1. Life in Thebes and Memphis
10   1. Knowledge from remains -- pictures, etc.
11   2. Houses high
12   3. Grain sorted by being thrown in air
13   4. Trinkets used for money
14   Age of Unification
15   1. Causes of:
16   A. Nile -- natural road-way, means of communication
17   B. Shut in from outsiders
18   C. Fertile country
19   (Diff. in case of Assyria. Euphrates open to
20   ingress.)

21 History of Euphrates Valley began after Egypt's civilization
22   1. First civilization in Egypt for reasons:
23   1. Desert, means of defense from barbarians
24   2. Climate - easy for primative people without means of
25   protection from cold -
26 II. History of Lower Valley of Euphrates.
27   1. As fertile as Nile Valley, but open to attack.
28   2. Elamites - overthrown 2000 B.C.
29   3. Supremacy of Babylon -
30   Commercial city in plains
31   a. Khammurabi
32   (Dec. 1901 - French excavating in Persia found
33   stone set up by Kham. with picture of King and
34   sun god -- and code of laws -- complete oldest
35   4. Assyrians
36   a. Recorded Babylonian literature
37   5. Medes - broke up Assyrian empire; control north.

When a student has notes like those on pages 188 & 189 he will frequently just give up on doing the G-B's.   This is a MAJOR MISTAKE. MAJOR MISTAKE.

Or, with notes like those which look nice and outlined, he will think the notes are clear enough for exam-review time.

    This is also a MAJOR MISTAKE. MAJOR MISTAKE. MAJOR...

To avoid the mistake:

    Start with ANY piece of Pie or any St-Pie Unit where you can figure out a G-B..

    ..Then make like you're working a jigsaw puzzle, getting a G-B here & a G-B there, from What's-in-your-head or What's-in-your-notes, and start fitting them together.

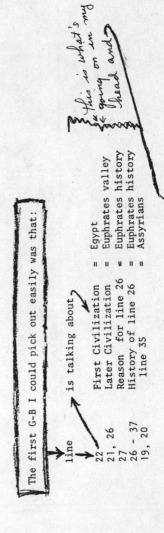

The first G-B I could pick out easily was that:

line	is talking about	
22	First Civilization	= Egypt
21, 26	Later Civilization	= Euphrates valley
27	Reason for line 26	= Euphrates history
26 - 37	History of line 26	= Euphrates history
19, 20	line 35	= Assyrians

this is what's going on in my head and

- civilizations
  - first = Egypt (Nile)
  - later = Euphrates
  - reason
  - history

I make scribble notes (?) like these as I go along - save wear & tear on my brains.

15 - 18	Reason for line 14 & 22	= Egypt & unification
11 - 13	Life in line 9	= Thebes & Memphis
10	Source of knowledge for line 9	= Thebes & Memphis
4 - 7	Source of knowledge for line 3	= Scientific method

going on in my head; and my

- civilizations
  - first = Egypt
    - reasons
    - life in Thebes...
      - source of knowledge
      - life there
  - source of knowledge of

scribble notes, you should make them, too.

that's
the best
I can do....

... this
jigsawing, finding
the G-B's, and
putting it all
together, is what the
School-people and
employers and parents call
"a challenge"...which is a polite word for a
lousy job you have to do.
It is also known as "studying".

Sept. 29 Professor Shotwell

Only former authority for knowledge of ancient world - Herodotus
and Bible
    Scientific Method
        1. Ancient stone -- key
Discovery of Rosetta stone, giving key to hieroglyphic & demotic
language opens up antique history -- 19th century, knowledge of
antiquity now gained by actual research

Egypt discovered solar year in 4241 B.C., July 19
    1. Life in Thebes and Memphis
        1. Knowledge from remains -- pictures, etc.
        2. Houses high
        3. Grain sorted by being thrown in air
        4. Trinkets used for money
    Age of Unification
        1. Causes of:
            A. Nile -- natural road-way, means of communication
            B. Shut in from outsiders
            C. Fertile country
                (Diff. in case of Assyria. Euphrates
                open to ingress.)

History of Euphrates Valley
    1. First civilization in Egypt for reasons:
        1. Desert, means of defense from barbarians
        2. Climate - easy for primative people without means of
            protection from cold -
   II. History of Lower Valley of Euphrates.
        1. As fertile as Nile Valley, but open to attack.
        2. Elamites - overthrown 2000 B.C.
        3. Supremacy of Babylon -
        Commercial city in plains
            a. Khammurabi
                (Dec. 1901 - French excavating in Persia found
                stone set up by Kham. with picture of King and
                sun god -- and code of laws -- complete oldest
        4. Assyrians
            a. Recorded Babylonian literature
        5. Medes - broke up Assyrian empire; control north.

ANCIENT WORLD
- Source of knowledge on it
    - formerly = Herodotus
                 &
                 Bible

Added in → I remembered this from the lecture.

    - present
        - Scientific method
            - Rosetta Stone discovery (1799 A.D.)
                - ancient stone in Euphrates Valley
                    - black basalt
                - "Trilingual" inscription
                    - hieroglyphics
                    - demotic language
                    - Greek language
                - key to ancient history
                    - 1st clue to deciphering Egyptian
        - actual research   hieroglyphics
            - study of ancient sites
            - carbon-dating of artifacts

- Civilizations
    - Earliest = Egypt
        - discovered Solar year (4241 B.C., July 19)
        - Life in Thebes & Memphis (cities)
            - source of knowledge
                - remains, pictures, etc.
            - life
                - houses high
                - grain sorted by being thrown in air
                - trinkets used for money
        - Reasons for Age of Unification & early civilization
            - Nile = natural roadway
                        means of communication
            - fertile country
            - shut in from outsiders
                - desert = defense from barbarians
    - Later = lower Euphrates Valley
        - reasons
            - fertile valley like Nile BUT OPEN TO ATTACK
        - History
            - Elamites = overthrown in 2000 B.C.
            - Babylon = supreme city
                - commercial city in plains
            - Code of Khammurabi = LAWS   *I put Statement first*
                - stone set up by Khammurabi
                    - picture of King
                                    Sun God
                                    the laws
                - oldest, most complete
                - discovered by French excavating group
                                                Dec. 1901
            - Assyrians
                - open to attack via Euphrates river
                - recorded Babylonian literature
                - Medes broke up the empire

You must fight off the compulsion to
start at the TOP of your notes & work
straight down the page...

Life isn't like that.
Start anywhere you can get a toe-hold on the material.

Remember, if you've been doing your
St-Pie sentence check-out for a
couple of weeks,

a lot of the G-B's will
already be in your notes.

What I usually do now
is a rough St-Pie of the G-B's.
This gives me a Summary of what
was covered in the lecture:

 AND I PUT A CHECK-MARK AGAINST
EACH ITEM AS I USE IT.

Don't be a nitwit about this.
Check off the items as you use them.
The check-off clears the air,
the page, &
your mind.

*Place date
in a corner
away from
content*

Sept. 29 (year)
Prof. Shotwell

Ancient World
- Source of knowledge on it
    - formerly
    - presently
        - Scientific method
        - actual research

*Question
mark
because the
meaning
of the two
items is
not clear
from notes.
Fuzzy area,
ask someone.*

(?)

- Civilizations of it
    - earliest = Egypt
        - life in cities
        - source of knowledge about it
        - reasons for it being first (3)

    - later = Euphrates Valley
        - reasons (1)
        - history (3 groups)

.... The St-Pie of the G-B's gives me some of
the exam questions...

which, if I can review for, and
answer, could get me a B grade?????

It could.
IF you follow this

PROCEDURE FOR TESTING WHAT YOU | DO NOT | NEED TO STUDY

1) Make up exam questions from the St-Pie of the G-B's

. What is the method(s) presently used to enlarge our
knowledge about the ancient world?

. Discuss the reasons for Egypt being the earliest
civilization in the ancient world.

. Which was the most important group of people to live
in the Euphrates valley? Why?

2) BEFORE you review your notes, scribble (abbreviate! or you
will waste time) your answers to about 5 or 10 of the
questions.

. By doing this you will learn

✔ what information is already coded into your brain
✔ the trick of making scribble notes DURING exams
✔ the technique of associative recall: notes to
question 9 jog off info for question 4

. However, if you answer a question and check with your
notes at the end of each answer

↳ you will only be fooling yourself...

. while you are checking one answer, your eyes
will be "reviewing" other notes on the page.

If you really know the answer,
it will take only two minutes
to scribble it onto paper.

If you really don't know it,
better find it out now than
during the exam ???

3) ⟶ next page, please.

3) When all questions are done, (the 5 or 10 referred to in
   step 2 above), check your scribbled, abbreviated answers
   against the information in your St-Pie notes,

AND YOU WILL FIND OUT
WHAT YOUR UNCONSCIOUS MIND
                                    HAS
                                          ALREADY
                                                MEMORIZED.

- Now, in your notes, check off the items you
  have answered correctly. This is material you
  know. Don't bother with it again. Do NOT
  re-read it again.

- With a colored crayon, mark the stuff you missed.
  Repeat steps 2 and 3, erasing the colored mark
  as you learn the material.

          This analysis of what-you-know and
          what-you-don't-know automatically
          makes you learn more material.

Please do not waste time re-learning what you already know.

   It is pitiful to see students re-memorizing stuff their
   minds have already memorized.
                    This causes sleepiness and
                    inability to concentrate.

For most students, more than half the
material has been memorized by the time
they have reached the level of St-Pieing the G-B's.

          When you have a St-Pie of the G-B's in
          your head (even if you call it by another
          name), you have what your teachers and
          employers mean by "understanding the stuff".

     This is what they mean when they
     say, "If you understand the material
     as you go along, you don't have to
     memorize for exams."

It's a lie.
You do have to memorize.

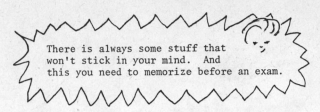

There is always some stuff that
won't stick in your mind. And
this you need to memorize before an exam.

NEW SUBJECT:

Has anyone ever explained to you how you can check out
whether you understand something correctly?

Or whether you have paraphrased something correctly?

Or whether you have outlined something correctly?

If you can't check out these things,
then you could be memorizing a lot of
incorrect stuff for exams....????

In the St-Pie system, you
check your understanding, or paraphrasing, or outlining
all in the same way

1) St-Pie the items
        &
        be sure you can make sensible sentences
        between the Statement & Pie items,
        using the Sentence Check-Out.

2) St-Pie the G-B's
        &
        be sure you can make sensible sentences
        between the Statement & Pie items,
        using the Sentence Check-Out.

                ..after all, a G-B is only another
                Statement. Pretty soon it just
                appears in your notes as St-Pie.

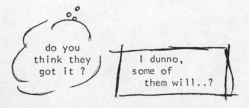

do you
think they
got it ?

I dunno,
some of
them will..?

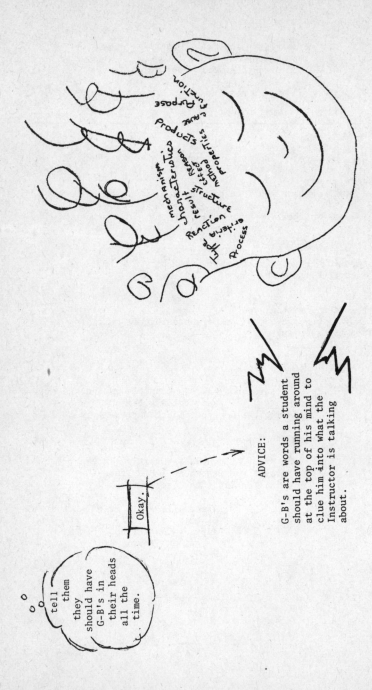

If a student's mind is on Life G-B's instead of School G-B's (while he is going to classes or studying) it will cause serious problems about "concentrating" on school work.

The next time you are not able to "concentrate" on your studies, take a look at which kind of G-B's are running around your head...

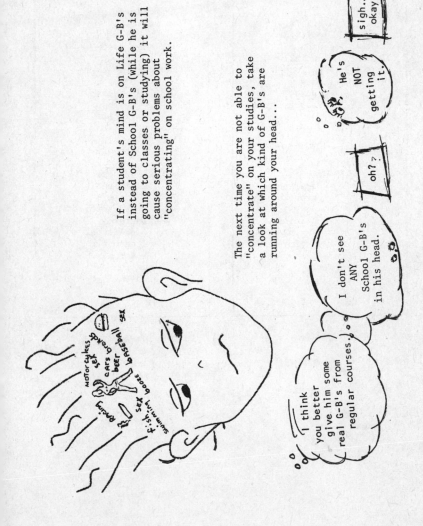

SOME   G-B's   FOR   SOME   COURSES ...

```
┌─────────────────────────────┐  ┌─────────────────────────────┐
│                             │  │                             │
│      HISTORY                │  │           SOCIOLOGY         │
│                             │  │                             │
│ - events                    │  │  - theory                   │
│    - types                  │  │     - leader                │
│       - non-military        │  │     - strength              │
│          - political        │  │     - weakness              │
│          - economic         │  │     - where used            │
│          - social           │  │                             │
│          - philosophical    │  │  - changes                  │
│       - military            │  │     - types                 │
│          - causes           │  │        - leaders            │
│          - results          │  │        - sources            │
│             - immediate     │  │        - results            │
│             - long range    │  │     - process               │
│                             │  │        - origin             │
│ - movements                 │  │        - stages             │
│    - types                  │  │                             │
│       - leaders             │  │  - Systems of social organiz.│
│          - doctrines        │  │     - classification        │
│          - strengths        │  │        - criteria for       │
│          - weaknesses       │  │        - characteristics    │
│          - policies         │  │     - structure             │
│             - internal      │  │        - political          │
│             - foreign       │  │        - economic           │
│       - causes              │  │        - social             │
│       - effects             │  │     - location              │
│                             │  │     - problems              │
│                             │  │        - types              │
│                             │  │                             │
└─────────────────────────────┘  └─────────────────────────────┘
```

G-B's are very inter-changeable words:

types = kinds
cause = origin

        reason = cause
        effects = results

                structure = composition
                purpose = function

```
ANATOMY

- name of something
    - type
    - structure
        - gross
        - microscopic
    - characteristics
        - physical
        - chemical
        - morphological
    - location
    - function
```

```
PHYSIOLOGY

- name of process (digestion, etc.)
    - type
    - structures involved
        - type
        - composition
            - gross
            - microscopic
    - properties (or characteristics)
    - mechanism to carry it out
        - physics changes
        - chemistry changes
    - functions
```

An extremely important use for the G-B's
is in making up CHARTS for a topic or
a course.

> Most people don't realize that a chart,
> made up from your notes and slot-ins,
> will pull the content together so you
> can COMPARE the stuff BEFORE YOU GET
> INTO THE EXAM.

Only geniuses have heads that can
put stuff together sideways and
up-and-down without using pencil
and paper. But most geniuses use
pencil and paper anyway. So do
very smart students.

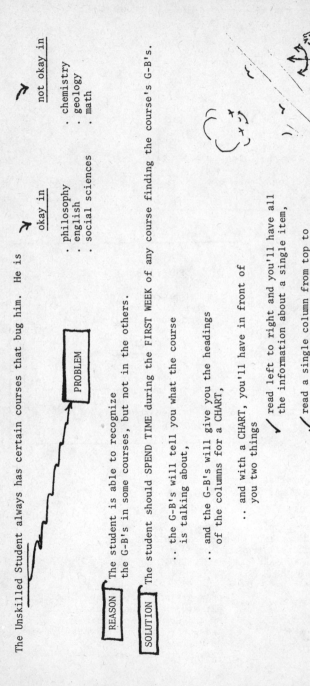

The Unskilled Student always has certain courses that bug him. He is

okay in

· philosophy
· english
· social sciences

not okay in

· chemistry
· geology
· math

PROBLEM

REASON   The student is able to recognize
the G-B's in some courses, but not in the others.

SOLUTION   The student should SPEND TIME during the FIRST WEEK of any course finding the course's G-B's.

.. the G-B's will tell you what the course
is talking about,

.. and the G-B's will give you the headings
of the columns for a CHART,

.. and with a CHART, you'll have in front of
you two things

read left to right and you'll have all
the information about a single item,

read a single column from top to
bottom, and you'll have the SIMILARITIES
and DIFFERENCES between the items.

These are the only types of factual-questions that can be asked on an exam.
If you can answer them, you can always get a B-grade without sweating the exam.

Be sure to PUT TITLES on EVERYTHING!   Title this one ⤸

203

SINGLE CHEMICAL REACTIONS →

REACTANTS	CATALYST (or conditions for reaction to take place)	PRODUCTS	PROCESS	TYPE OF REACTION	NAME OF REACTION
$C + O_2$ carbon=1 atom oxygen=2 atoms	heat	CO_2 carbon dioxide	oxidation	combination	this may be the
H_2O (water) molecule & electric current	liquid state of H_2O	$H_2 + 1/2\ O_2$ hydrogen + 1/2 oxygen molecule	electrolysis	dissociation	name of a person.

In all courses, and for all Charts,
watch out for different words that have the same meaning.

Sometimes the Instructor uses them.

Sometimes the texts use them.

This "different word" bit can land you a double
whammy in courses like Philosophy. But you are
not to panic. Follow these directions

FIRST: Make a list of the G-B's that you hear
over & over...like the capitalized words below ↙

Every PHILOSOPHER uses some TYPE OF REASONING to go from ARGUMENT to CONCLUSION.

SECOND: Make a rough, abbreviated chart using these G-B's

phil.	Rea.	Arg.	Concl.

THIRD: Look at the left-overs, the miscellaneous G-B's that only
showed up once or twice in various lectures or textbooks ↙

These words all mean the same thing in your mind

"This is what the guy starts out with and says you have to accept without any proof."

The miscellaneous G-B's ——> Philosopher A starts out with an ASSUMPTION
                          Philosopher B   "   "   "   " PRESUPPOSITION
                          Philosopher C   "   "   "   " AXIOM
                          Philosopher D   "   "   "   " PREMISE

So...make up a [G-B] of your own that will include all of them
and call it [STARTING POINT]

Now CHART the material, using your G-B as the column heading, and their G-B's as the column content.

COMPARISON OF PHILOSOPHIES ← title

PHILOSOPHER	STARTING POINT	TYPE OF REASONING	ARGUMENT	CONCLUSION about Self..Man..Universe..	MY CRITICISM of his argument
A	Assumption: St-Pie it	inductive (pie → st)			no Pie for St #2
B	Presupposition: St-Pie it	deductive (st → pie)			incorrect Pie for St #1
C	Axiom: St-Pie it	both (pie → st) (st → pie)			contradictory Pie for St #3 & 6

To train yourself to listen
and hear the G-B's,

ALWAYS TAKE DOWN EVERYTHING THE
INSTRUCTOR SAYS IN THE FIRST FIVE
MINUTES OF A LECTURE,

.. he may be reviewing the
   lecture of yesterday.

.. he may be previewing the
   lecture of today.

.. Review or Preview, it will
   have his own pet G-B's in it.

AND

ALWAYS TAKE DOWN EVERYTHING THE
INSTRUCTOR SAYS IN THE LAST FIVE
MINUTES OF A LECTURE.

.. he may be giving a summary of
   today's lecture.

.. he may be giving a preview of
   tomorrow's lecture.

.. Summary or Preview, it will
   have his own pet G-B's in it.

FOR EXAMPLE

Somewhere, sometime..at the beginning or
ending of some lecture..the Instructor's voice
will say something like this: ⌐

" The next lectures will be primarily devoted to the
relationship of the structure of protein molecules
to their biological roles. Proteins will be
discussed in terms of their size, shape, conformation,
primary structure, catalytic mechanism and
regulatory properties."

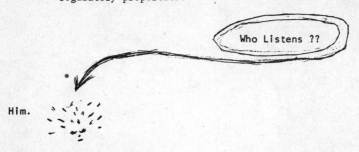

Who Listens ??

Him.

One student is
scribbling in his notebook
like all the demons of hell
are after him.

That night, peaceful & smug,
he St-Pies what the Instructor
said: " The next topic will be... "

PROTEIN MOLECULES
    - Structures
            - size
            - shape
            - conformation
            - primary structure
    - catalytic mechanism that makes
                    \ molecules work
    - Function
            - regulatory properties
            - biological roles

Very nice...very nice indeed...all the G-B's for that topic
       anyway...nice G-B's...Nice chart headings...
                           nice movie in town tonight...

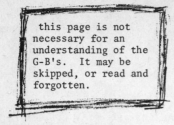

this page is not
necessary for an
understanding of the
G-B's. It may be
skipped, or read and
forgotten.

It is very soul-satisfying to hold onto the moment
of freedom before you settle in to listen to the
Instructor -- selecting out your pens, opening your
notebook, snapping an exquisitely clean sheet of
paper into your clip-board, smiling a comradely
smile at the female sitting beside you.

And when the hour is ending, while the Instructor's
voice is still droning away, there is a gentle sense of
power as you pocket your pens, and close your notebook,
and gather up your things from the floor, in preparation for
your next moment of freedom.

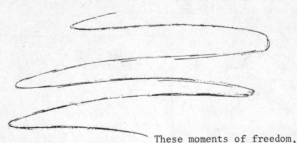

These moments of freedom,

oh Student-not-wise-in-the-ways-of-learning,

can cost you hours of work.

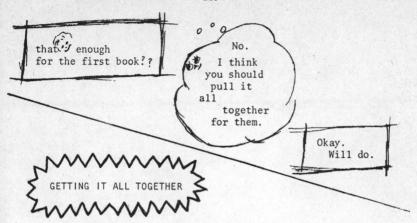

It is always a Good Thing
to scribble in the margins of texts or notebooks
a rough idea of the G-B's for the
large chunks of the content → like [the paragraphs
&
the sections

This affects your mind in two ways:

. your mind forms a skeleton outline of the content,
which gets "fleshed out" when you read the stuff.

. your mind recognizes stuff it already knows from
some other book, or some other lecture.
(..and there's no point in reading that again!)

Get it through your skull
that you are not a Scholar.
Only Scholars read seventeen
sources on the same material. That is their business.

Your business is to get a
simple, clear picture
of the content. That's all.

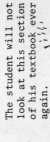

Another Good Thing is to use
a pencil when you scribble your G-B's, because
         as the picture gets clearer,
         the G-B's change..
                  G
                clump..
                  G
                other moveable actions..

When the G-B's are scribbled,
then
decide what you are going to do with the stuff. You will

- St-Pie it
- make a chart of it
- sketch it
- or forget it

On the next pages
is an example of how a student "read" part of a textbook:

  .. the G-B's are in the margin

  .. what he decided to do with the material
    is written in a circle beside the material

  .. and his Selective St-Pie notes (charts, visuals, St-Pies)
    are on the same page.

The student will not
look at this section
of his textbook ever
again.

– SELECTIVE ST-PIE OF A TEXTBOOK* –

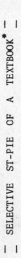

RESPIRATION -- a life process common to all living things

Each living cell takes in oxygen, uses it in the oxidation of foods, and gives off carbon dioxide and water. This vital process supplies the cell with energy to carry on its life processes.

We can define respiration as the intake of oxygen and the elimination of carbon dioxide associated with energy release in living cells.

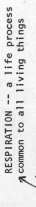

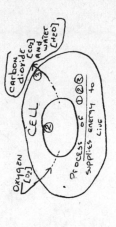

*Modern Biology by James H. Otto and Albert Towle, copyright © 1969 by Holt, Rinehart and Winston, Inc. Reprinted by permission of the publisher.

(continued on next pages, please.)

Types of Respiration

Loc. of type	Process that goes on during each type
Simple org. Ex- jellyfish	direct xchange of gases betw cell + environment
Insects	direct xchange of gases via Trachea Air → trach → tissues
More complicated animals Ex. Man	indirect xchange of gases — O₂ → tissues — needs a mechanism

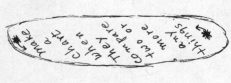

Types of Resp →

In some of the simple organisms such as the protists, sponges, and jellyfish, the cells are in direct contact with the environment, and an exchange of gases between the cells and their surroundings occurs directly. Plant cells also respire in this way. In an insect, air is delivered directly to the tissues through the tracheae. However, as animals become more complicated in their structures the cells are deprived of direct contact with the external environment. Some means of receiving oxygen at one place and carrying it to the body tissues becomes necessary.

External Respiration

Air → Lungs → Blood → body tissues

Breathing gas transported exchange

external respiration

internal respiration

Breathing + External Respir. } Organs

Passageway organs — Air → bloodstream

Breathing organs — mechanical change size of chest cavity

← title? add...

visual

St-Pie or visual

Phases of Resp.

Two phases of respiration in man.

Ext. Resp.

External respiration is the exchange of gases between the atmosphere and the blood. This phase involves the lungs. Internal respiration is the exchange of gases between the blood and the body tissues. It occurs in every living cell. Breathing is merely a mechanical process involved in getting the air to and from the lungs.

structures (organs) in resp.

We can divide the organs concerned with breathing and external respiration into two groups. The first group includes the passages through which air travels in reaching the bloodstream. The second group is concerned with the mechanics of breathing, that is, with changing the size of the chest cavity.

Process
of → Gas exchange in the lungs;

The pulmonary artery
brings dark red (deoxy-
genated) blood to the
lungs. There, it divides
into an extensive
network of capilla-
ries, completely sur-
rounding each air sac.
The thin, moist walls of
both air sac and cap-
illary permit the rapid
gaseous exchange of
oxygen from air to
blood and of carbon di-
oxide and water from
blood to air. The
pulmonary veins return
to the heart the
bright red (oxygenated)
blood for the tissues.

Visual + St.-Pie

Blood Flow Thru Lung System

Lung
heart
blood
Pulmonary Artery
capillaries
Air Sac
Pulmonary Vein
heart

① dark red blood
 - deoxygenated
 - into capillaries

② bright rd blood
 - oxygenated
 - for tissues

③ exchange made
 between air sacs +
 capillaries

Air sac ⎫ walls
capillary ⎭
 - thin
 - moist
 - allow gas exchange
 O_2 in air q blood →
 $CO_2 + H_2O$ in blood → air

..Here

NOTE TO STUDENTS: The heading is Gas exchange...etc. But the CONTENT is actually talking about
 two things: (1) the gas exchange..see dotted line area of text; and (2) the
 blood flow through lung system. This is somewhat confused writing, but
 clarifies with the use of G-B's. The Visual has one title; it needs a second one.

Another way of sketching stuff like
the material in the "Gas exchange..." heading
is to make a line-diagram and St-Pie along the side of the lines.

ANY KIND OF VISUAL THAT WORKS
FOR YOU IS OKAY.

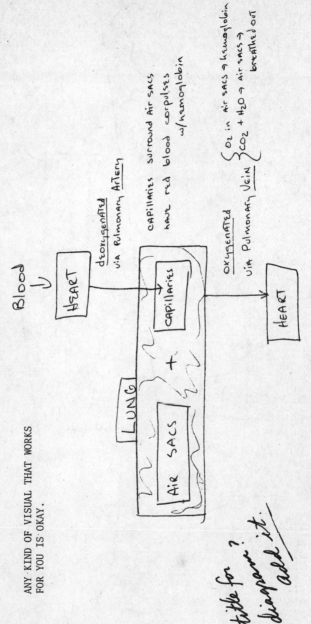

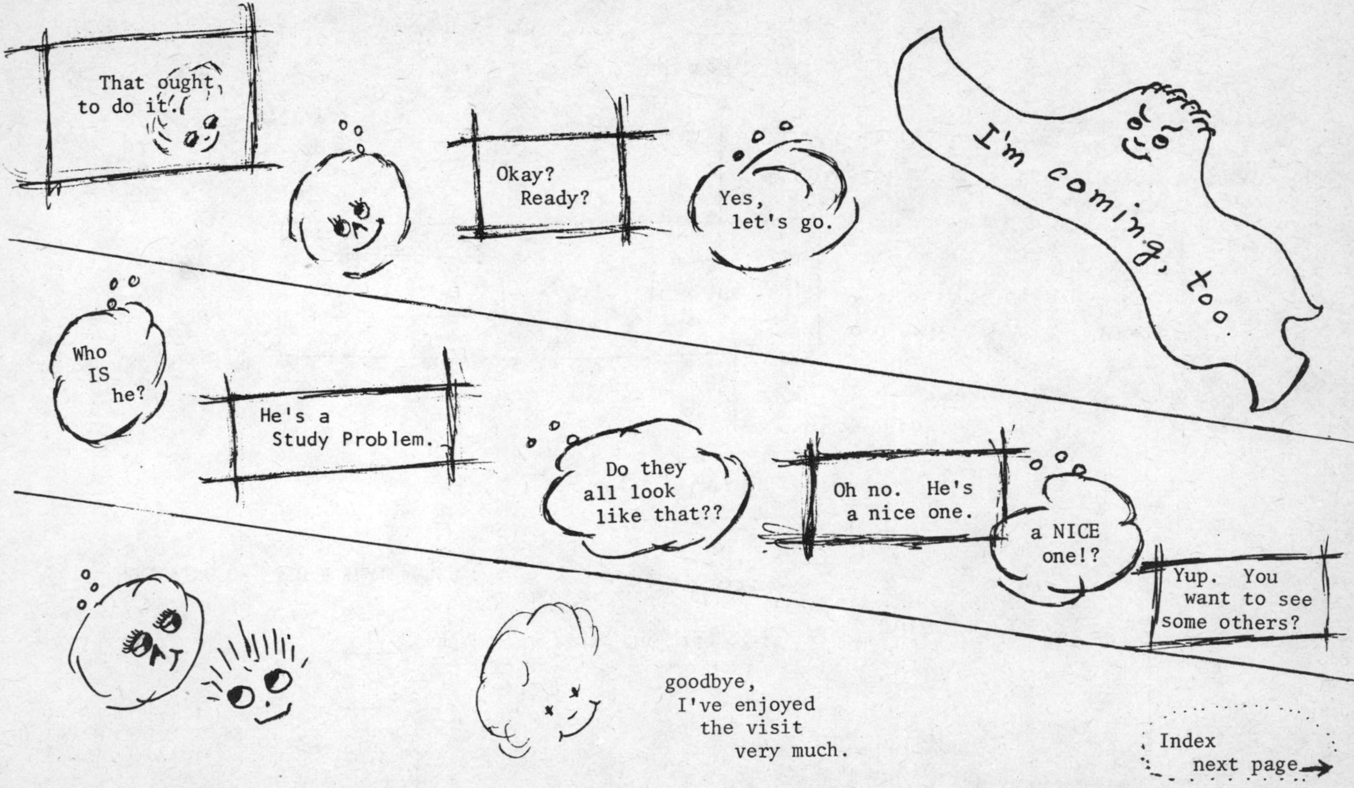
That ought to do it!
Okay? Ready?
Yes, let's go.
I'm coming, too.
Who IS he?
He's a Study Problem.
Do they all look like that??
Oh no. He's a nice one.
a NICE one!?
Yup. You want to see some others?
goodbye, I've enjoyed the visit very much.
Index next page

INDEX

74 75 76 77 10 9 8 7 6 5 4 3 2